HIGH*lights*

Modern musings on
ancient wisdom

Rebbetzen Shuli Liss

In loving memory of our dear grandparents:

Yonah and Devorah Stemmer
Dr Shmuel and Bertl Katz
Sam and Cecilia Jay
Hyman and Edith Liss

We are here today because of the
choices they made many years ago.

Written by Rebbetzen Shuli Liss
Edited by: Annabel Ries
Project Manager: Laurie Resnick
Fundraising: Debbie Fox

Design: Richard Herman, www.hermie.co.uk
Printed by: City Printing, www.cityprintingltd.co.uk
Images: Shutterstock and Richard Herman

First published in Great Britain in 2022 by the United Synagogue,
305 Ballards Lane, Finchley, London N12 8GB
Registered charity number 242552
info@theus.org.uk
www.theus.org.uk

ISBN 978-1-909004-17-7

CONTENTS

בס"ד

Office of The
CHIEF RABBI

Message from the Chief Rabbi

Referring to the Torah, our Sages declare (Avot 5:25) "Hafoch ba vahafoch ba dekula ba" – turn it this way and that and you will discover that it contains everything!

This notion is illustrated masterfully by Rebbetzen Shuli Liss in the gems she conveys in this wonderful book. Drawing on a wealth of Torah sources, she shows how, whatever the subject, our tradition guides and inspires us through all of life's experiences.

The Highgate community is truly blessed to have a Rebbetzen of the exceptional calibre of Rebbetzen Liss. I extend my best wishes for continuous beracha vehatzlacha – blessing and success, to her and Rabbi Liss within the Highgate community and well beyond.

Chief Rabbi Ephraim Mirvis
February 2022 • Adar I 5782

Introduction

Have you ever driven to a place on auto pilot and wondered how you got there?

That is how I feel right now. Here I am, writing an introduction to a book that I never planned to write.

I started writing Shabbat messages to the community a few years ago, on an ad-hoc basis. Here and there, when I had time, I penned some thoughts that I hoped would be relevant and would help members to feel closer to our community and to Hashem.

Over time, I wrote more often. Then, when Covid hit, it became my primary way of connecting with the community and hopefully giving them messages of hope and encouragement during these difficult times.

We are all human and, interestingly enough, I have found that whilst our successes are often shared on social media, it is our failures and struggles that unite us. When we open up and share our difficulties and how we have grown or survived through them, we invite others to learn from our experiences.

I have tried to be honest and open in my writing. My life is still very much a work in progress, and I don't profess to have mastered any of the lessons discussed in the book. The Torah's wisdom is for all of us, and when I wrote those messages each week, I was also talking to myself. My hope is that the words inscribed in this book will help us, together, to learn, grow and improve in our relationship with Hashem and with each other.

> *Living life with meaning, purpose and a close relationship with Hashem infuses one with hope.*

We chose the title "HIGHlights" because, to me, the word symbolises the idea of looking up **high** for inspiration and bringing that **light** to the world.

When we look up to Hashem for guidance, our lives are transformed from a daily grind to moments of incredible potential for growth. Living life with meaning, purpose and a close relationship with Hashem infuses one with hope, no matter what the day brings.

The word "High" also connects me to the Highgate Shul community, which we have been privileged to be a part of for the last 13 years. Highgate Shul is a warm, fun and caring place to be, and I love our community dearly.

When I was asked to write an introduction, I looked at the introductions of a few books at home to find some inspiration. In the introduction to Dr Wikler's book "Aishel: Stories of Contemporary Jewish Hospitality", he wrote how he had experienced first-hand hospitality from a variety of people over the years, and how he has welcomed people into his home too. When asked by his guests how they could repay his kindness, he told them that the greatest gift they could give him would be to pass on the kindness to someone else and open their home to guests.

I thought that this is a beautiful idea, and it is my request to you too. If you find any of the messages inspiring, please share them with others.

A man once approached Rabbi Schneerson, the Lubavitcher Rebbe, to obtain a blessing from him. The Rabbi asked him if he taught anyone some Torah. The man replied that he was not knowledgeable enough to teach. Rabbi Schneerson asked, "Do you know the Hebrew alphabet?" The man replied "Yes". "So, teach someone else those holy letters!"

We all have something to give and teach, and the world needs teachers and educators to inspire the next generation. Any Torah idea that you share will bring merit to yourself and the world.

Hashem created this world, and maintains it every minute, whilst simultaneously hiding behind the scenes, to enable human beings to have free will and do our part to perfect it. Hashem waits patiently for the world to realise and acknowledge this. The Jewish people's mission is to follow the Torah's laws as best as we can, and thereby inspire the world.

May these words touch your soul, and together, may we merit to uplift and inspire all those around us.

Rebbetzen Shuli Liss
Highgate, January 2022

Acknowledgements

Tere are too many people I need to thank, so here is a brief list. For all those not mentioned by name, please forgive me and I thank you from the bottom of my heart for all your editing, feedback, and inspiration.

First of all, thank you to all those who donated towards the publication of this book. I am humbled by your generosity.

If you enjoy this book, it is thanks to Brian Gardner for suggesting to me that we compile the weekly messages that I send out the community into a book for the wider public to enjoy (and hopefully learn from). At first, I was touched by the idea. But after many hours of work, I now realise that was not quite as easy as it sounded! Thank you, Brian. It is in your merit.

As with all good ideas, we need help moving a concept from theory into practice. Thank you to Adam Leigh for helping lay down the ground-work and for your encouragement with the project. Together with your co-chair (and my loyal friend) Kate Bearman, you sowed the seeds for this book to happen.

Our incredible co-chair, Debbie Fox, managed the fundraising, whilst simultaneously adjusting to a whole new world of Shul commitments, with Covid complications and a changeover of administration. Debbie has been an invaluable source of support and advice since she joined our team, and I am indebted to her for so much more than helping create this book.

In 2017, I began writing occasional messages to the women of the community. Claire Hilton was a co-chair at the time and she continually encouraged me to write more. Pressing the 'Send' button was (and still is) a scary event for me, but throughout the last few years Claire has given me reassurance, helpful feedback and guidance for many of the articles. Both Robin and Claire spent many hours looking over the manuscript, and I am so grateful for their advice, support and friendship.

Thank you to Laurie Resnick, from the United Synagogue Living and Learning team, for managing the project, Richard Herman for his wonder-ful graphic design, and Annabel Ries for her efficient and insightful editing. It was a pleasure working with such a professional, yet patient, team.

Most weeks, I sent my articles to our children to read over and comment upon, before emailing them out to the community. Their honest (sometimes brutally honest) feedback has kept me in check, and I am so grateful to them for their patience and honesty. The chapters that are not in this book are a credit to their wisdom and sensitivity.

My wonderful parents and parents in laws have encouraged and supported me for so many years. Their advice and enthusiasm have given me the confidence to keep writing, even as I felt unworthy to do so. My dearest siblings, too, have helped and inspired me with their wisdom and actions, and also sent me some inspirational ideas worth sharing.

To those of you who read my messages over the past few years and commented, thank you for your feedback – both positive and negative. In particular, thanks to Tim Cowen, Gerald Beverly and David Lewis for their helpful and meaningful feedback. One of the perks of my job is that I have the opportunity to learn from all our members and from the other people I meet. From your responses, culled from your varied experiences and outlooks, I have gained a greater appreciation and understanding of humankind.

Being a Rabbi is more than a full-time job – he doesn't even get a day of rest! Yet, despite his incredibly full schedule, my dear husband still made the time to check, look up and correct my many mistakes. Thank you for all your support and encouragement, always.

Lastly, 'Acharon Acharon Chaviv', the last is the most precious: thank You Hashem, my Creator and Sustainer, who has given me the ability to think, learn, talk and write. Every minute of my life is a miracle, a gift from up above, and if it were not for Hashem's constant support and love, I would not be here writing today.

When Helping is Not Helpful

JANUARY 2017

We all like to help. It is a basic trait and one that most of us would find praiseworthy in a person. But there are times when helping is not helpful.

Let me share with you a typical scenario in a family home.

"Mummy, can you get me... Can you help me clean this up ... Can you help me solve this problem?"

So, my usual response (I'd like to think) is, "Sure, darling. I'm here for you".

Sometimes though, I end up cleaning up the mess, working on the homework or solving the problem myself. This is not at all helpful. What have I taught the children?

1. Mummy can solve my problems.
2. I cannot.

Some of you may be thinking, I don't have young kids, so this isn't relevant to me. But it is relevant to all of us as we interact with others every day. Even if they are not our children, we can help many different people in life – but first we need to double check inside: is this really helpful for them or not?

The Torah guides us how to really help. In Parshat Mishpatim (Exodus 23:15), Hashem gives us some instructions. Imagine you are walking down a street and there you see a person (actually it says "your enemy", but that's another lesson) with his donkey overloaded. The verse says "You shall surely help with him".

> *We need to think carefully before offering help, to ensure that it is in the best interest of the recipient.*

'With' is the operative word in this sentence.

Help the person to help themselves. Don't do it for them, but rather offer encouragement and help alongside. The problem still belongs to the other, but now it is shared, and you are on their side. If the person has no intention of dealing with it at all, then helping them only perpetuates the problem.

I don't need to take care of a problem if I can ask someone else and they will do it. This does not teach personal responsibility. It can even make the person feel worse about themselves.

So, from now on, I will try to notice when I want to jump in to help, and instead take a step back. "Hmm... I see this is problem; how do you think we can solve this one?" is a much healthier response.

A friend mentioned to me that this generation is the 'snowflake' generation, with young adults finding it difficult to handle situations as they were 'helped' too much along their life journey so far.

Maimonides writes that the highest form of charity is to help another person to find a job and thereby become self-sufficient. It isn't easy to let go, and it feels nice to give of ourselves. But ultimately we need to think carefully before offering help, to ensure that it is in the best interest of the recipient.

I hope that you found this helpful and that all our help will be truly beneficial to all those around us.

A Different Key

PARSHAT VAYERA, NOVEMBER 2017

I am a list person. There is lots to do and I find that making a list helps me keep track of what needs to be done. But there are downsides to lists.

When we are focused on our own agendas and what we need to complete before the day is done, we may miss out on really understanding or relating to people. When our minds are task oriented, then time is more pressured, and our patience levels are low.

Yesterday, I had several meetings and jobs to finish. I may have successfully completed them, but at the end of the day I didn't feel good. Life isn't one big list. It contains people and feelings and beautiful moments, but I had missed those as I rushed through the day like it was an episode of "The Crystal Maze".

In Parshat Vayera, Abraham is sitting at the entrance to his tent, recuperating from his circumcision. He sees some Arab men walking towards him. They then stop and stand there, at a distance. The verse says "he looked" again. Rashi (1040–1105, one of the most influential Jewish commentators) explains that Abraham looked again to try to understand why they were standing there. Then he understood. They felt bad to bother him, so they waited far away so as not to disturb him.

> *Abraham wasn't thinking of himself or of his plan for the day. He looked out and thought of others.*

Abraham became the great person he was because he looked again. He looked further... what do they need? Why are they standing there?

Abraham wasn't thinking of himself or of his plan for the day. He looked out and thought of others.

Nechama Cohen is a modern young Jewish singer. One of her songs is called "A Different Key". It talks of how we all sing our own song but wonders how beautiful it would be if we could all join along, "together in unison, listening to every note".

How wonderful it would be if we could stop our song occasionally and be there to listen fully to someone else's song.

QUESTIONS TO THINK ABOUT:

- *Do you feel heard?*
- *When someone asks how you are, do you think they want to hear the honest answer?*
- *Are you a list person? Can you sometimes stop and put away your agenda and truly be there for another person?*
- *How can we practise taking a "second look"?*
- *Reading between the lines, what does the other person need?*

A Different Key (extract)

I'm trying to talk, but it seems nobody's here
Everyone's around but they won't stop to care
I just wanna be heard but no one's listening
The more I try, my voice is fading

Everyone's singing but they're singing their own song
Why can't we all join along?
Together in harmony, listening to every note

If we blend our voices together in unison
We can make beautiful music
Don't sing too loud or you might miss out

On some other great melody
Even if it's in a different key
Everyone's busy, they don't want to hear

How my day was, and why I went where
Living their own lives, oblivious
Not realizing how much they're missing

Tune into what others are saying to you
There'll be so much more awaiting you
There's a lot you can learn it's not hard to find
If you open your mind.

Selfless Giving

PARSHAT SHEMOT, JANUARY 2018

When our children or students succeed, we feel a natural pride. We pat ourselves on the back, or others congratulate us and we feel proud of their achievements. Those feelings are normal, but we may need to question our motives in this competitive world. Is that 'A' on the report card for her or for me? Is that particular school best for him or best for my feelings of pride? We have hopes and goals for our children and students, but do they truly take into account the person's individual talents and aspirations or are we using them as extensions of ourselves?

People often come over to me and say how lovely our children are. I am so grateful to Hashem that they are indeed good children, but I normally answer that they are individual gifts from heaven. I cannot take the credit for their sweetness (as I would then have to take responsibility for any of their behaviours that I may not like). Each human being has free choice and our job is to help them grow in their own path, not for our nachas.

In Parshat Shemot, we read the story of how Moses was born, put in the Nile and watched over by his sister, and looked after by the daughter of Pharaoh. If we study the language of the text, we notice that no actual names are given for all those involved in his upbringing: "a woman and a man, from the house of Levi had a child", "his sister" watched, two Jewish midwives with pseudonyms looked after him, the daughter of Pharaoh is not named...

Our rabbis explain that part of the process to help Moses become the person who led 600,000 people was that he was brought up by selfless people. They weren't interested in themselves and their own dreams for this child – they gave to Moses purely for his sake. His sister watched from the side of the river at great personal danger to ensure his survival. The daughter of Pharaoh took in a Jewish child despite her father's orders to kill them all.

Each human being has free choice and our job is to help them grow in their own path, not for our nachas.

As Moses is brought up in the King's palace, the verse writes that "the lad grew". He didn't just grow physically; he grew spiritually. How? The next verse describes his greatness: "he went out to his brothers". He was safe in the palace and was treated like a prince, yet he went out to see what he could do to help those outside the palace gates.

He learnt through the selfless giving of those who helped him in his childhood, and this gave him the ability to empathise and become a person who could care for and lead the Jewish nation.

We all have influence over others in our life and it is natural to be delighted with their achievements. Maybe, sometimes, we need to double check our motives. Do we measure ourselves by their success or failure? Or do we allow them to follow their own unique path and assist them with their own goals?

For me, it's still a work in progress, as I hope and pray for the growth and success of all those I meet.

What's Done is Done

JANUARY 2018

"What's done is done."
Macbeth Act 3, Scene 2

Every time I press the 'Send' button to share my 'Reflections' email with the community I get a nervous feeling. Is this good enough? Might I have offended someone in it? Maybe I wrote something wrong? This is now going to be sent out to over two hundred people. Yikes!

We all experience self-doubt.
Should I have said that?
If only I hadn't done that, then I wouldn't be in this position!
I could've done it, but I didn't...

These thoughts of regret can be helpful and yet are sometimes harmful. We cannot live in the past; whatever is done was done.

In Judaism, we have a concept called 'bashert'. It's meant to be. It's not

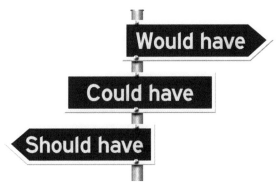

an easy concept when we are beating ourselves up for something we did wrong, but it is one that can help us learn how to move on in our life.

Everything that happens in this world is meant to be. Even the pain and even the mistakes we make. Hashem runs the world. Although of course, that doesn't preclude our responsibility to do the right thing.

Before any action, we need to think it through and make sure that it is fulfilling Hashem's will. Am I making this world a better place with my actions? Are these words kind and loving? Is there another way to achieve this goal without hurting anyone?

We admit our faults, decide and plan how to change, apologise to the person we hurt and Hashem, and then we move on.

However, once we have hit the 'Send' button, we need to let go. I cannot undo the past, and now I need to trust myself and look forward.

If we have made a mistake, then we are required to make amends. Hashem, in mercy, has given us the process of 'teshuva'. By doing true teshuva, we admit our faults, decide and plan how to change, apologise to the person we hurt and Hashem, and then we move on.

Guilt and shame aren't helpful. They only hold us back from dealing with the present and trying to do what is best now.

Someone once taught me that the way to measure whether a thought or feeling is helpful is to see what mood it puts me in. If I am sad and frustrated with myself, I won't achieve anything. But if I accept myself and my mistakes lovingly, then I will take whatever steps are needed to correct the error and change those faulty character traits.

What's done is bashert. What I do now is my free choice.

The Small Things

MARCH 2018

*"Never in the field of human conflict has so much been
owed by so many to so few"*

Winston Churchill

Sometimes we read about great people, or we hear about huge accomplishments that others have achieved in their lives. We may wonder, what about me? Am I actually making any difference in this large world with billions of people?

The truth is that each one of us has the power to make a huge difference in other people's lives and it doesn't have to be a huge effort to bring some light to another's day.

Recently, a beautiful group of pre-Bat Mitzva girls and their mothers came to learn together at Shul. I love that age, as the girls are open to learning and bring a lovely, positive energy to the Shul.

Each girl brought with them a small item that reminded them of some Chessed (kindness) that others had done for them and had made a difference to their lives. The mothers and daughters shared their own stories, and I was so inspired by those small (and sometimes large) acts of kindness that brought joy to their lives, even years later.

A few weeks ago, I was stopped by a lady in a shop a few hours before Shabbat. She was hurrying out of the shop, with bags in each hand . "You won't remember me, but I had a lovely Shabbat with you when I was in Seminary in Israel many years ago. I just wanted to say thank you".

She was right, I didn't remember her (I'm not so good at remembering people – forgive me!). Yet through the whole of Shabbat I kept on remembering her words and feeling so happy that she actually remembered that occasion and that someone enjoyed being with us for Shabbat over ten years ago. It was a passing comment as she rushed off to finish her shopping, but the warm feeling stayed with me for a lot longer.

Parshat Eikev says "What does Hashem ask from you? Just to serve Hashem and walk humbly in His ways". The Torah isn't asking us to accomplish huge things and totally change our lives – just walk humbly in Hashem's ways.

Whoever said the small things don't matter has never seen a match start a wildfire.

Every day we have opportunities to cheer up someone else. A small compliment. A call to say hello, or a text to show you care.

It's just a small thought, but as the writer Beau Taplin said:

"Whoever said the small things don't matter has never seen a match start a wildfire".

A Time to Cry

APRIL 2018

I dread looking at the news. I know it needs to be done, as we all need to be aware of what is happening around us in the world. Yet, I dread checking it and seeing the terrible events taking place.

Recently, there have been pictures of people injured from the chemical warfare attacks in Syria. Many of those injured and killed were women and children. Innocent women and children. Mothers, daughters and sisters like us.

The other night, the headline on the BBC news was "Are we heading for a third world war?" Ties between Russia and America are worrisome, and the world seems to be in quite a precarious position.

I am not writing to scare you, or to start a political discussion, as this is not at all my area of expertise. I am writing because I think it is a time to pray.

How often do we read the news, shake our heads, and continue with our day? We cannot cry every time we read the paper, yet we cannot just move on without letting this information touch us in some way.

It is hard to cry for someone else's pain. We need to put our hearts into their world and imagine how they are feeling. It takes emotional effort. And anyway, does it even make a difference?

On Pesach we remember how we were taken out of Egypt and saved from slavery. In the Haggada, we recite the story of how the Exodus took place. We recall the difficult work and the oppression, and then the Haggada writes "and they cried out" to Hashem (Exodus 2:23).

We were in Egypt for 210 years and we could not leave. Only when we cried did Hashem took us out.

Right now, thank G-d, we are living in a safe country. We lock our doors at night and can sleep comfortably in our own homes. The news features are on our screens, but we can easily ignore them and tell ourselves that things aren't so bad. In Egypt, the people became accustomed to their lives, and some didn't even want to leave.

Can we melt our hearts just for a few moments to pray for those suffering?

In Judaism, we believe that Hashem counts every tear. Every heartfelt prayer, in any language. Can we melt our hearts just for a few moments to pray for those suffering? To beg Hashem to bring Mashiach and peace to the world? Hashem values every word and cry from our hearts. It has the power to uproot many difficult decrees. Every individual can make a difference to the experience of the world through their prayer and their tears.

I am sorry if this message is a little heavy, but I feel that in order for us to lead happy and productive lives, we sometimes shut off (so to speak) our hearts so that we can move on after reading terrible news. This might be a necessary protection mechanism, but at times we need to switch our hearts back on.

If we can only open those hearts for a few minutes each day to really feel what we are reading and cry out from our pain, we may be able to help avert more tragedies to come.

A Treasure for You

SHAVUOT, MAY 2018

Imagine I asked you to do me a favour. How would you respond?

It would be normal for you to ask me what I would like you to do before saying yes. How can you say yes if you don't know what you are expected to do?

Now, imagine instead that I ask if I could give you a gift. Well, that's a bit different. We often accept gifts without knowing what's inside and then, only after we unwrap it, do we see whether we like it.

A gift benefits the recipient. A favour benefits the person who requests it.

In a couple of days, we celebrate Shavuot, where Hashem gave us the gift of the Torah. We accepted it with open arms, with the words "Na'aseh venishma", we will do and we will listen.

Gift? Is the Torah really a gift? It's full of laws and rules. A box of chocolates sounds nicer!

Some people feel that we are doing Hashem a favour by keeping the Torah. It makes Hashem happy. Yet, the honest truth is that this large book of laws and stories is the greatest gift that we could ever receive. Why?

Because it is actually a treasure map. If we follow its instructions, we will find the treasure of a life of inner peace and fulfilment. Gd created us and this world, and the Torah is our guide to help us through the maze of life.

> *A gift benefits the recipient. A favour benefits the person who requests it.*

To be clear, it's not an easy treasure map. It involves time and effort and learning and working on ourselves. We, the Jewish people, were given this treasure map and it sits in our homes on a bookshelf.

How often do we stop to study it? It's worth more than gold but it's gathering dust.

I'm talking to myself here. Even though I try to live by its laws, I rarely take the time to open up the Torah and learn it with the commentaries or, even better, with a chavruta (learning partner). When I do manage to carve out that time, I feel inspired and energized and promise myself that I must do this more often.

Hashem loves us and gave us the Torah for our benefit. It is true that Hashem is pleased when we learn and keep it, but that's more like when a parent is pleased to see a child succeed. Hashem wants the best for us, and is sad to see us stumble along life without its guidance.

This Shavuot, let us dust off that precious book and take it down from the shelf.

Maybe come to one of our learning sessions or attend a different one in your neighbourhood.

If you are busy on Shavuot, then there are plenty of other opportunities to learn during the week. The internet is full of inspiring Torah lessons, at the click of a button.

Whichever way you choose to connect with our Creator, I wish you a beautiful, meaningful Shavuot with a slice of delicious cheesecake too!

How Are You Feeling?

JUNE 2018

Have you ever wondered why some people are so easy-going and nothing seems to bother them? They calmly deal with any problems and don't get het up when things don't go their way.

The rest of us, though, often find ourselves furious, devastated or elated about life's ups and downs.

When our daughter told me she had passed her driving test, she had to hold the phone far away from her ears as I was squealing so loudly and dancing with delight. On the other hand, I'm not such great company when I'm upset. I am working on it.

We are taught in the Torah that every single person has a purpose in

this world. All our character traits can be used for the good or the bad. The choice is ours. Those of us who feel things strongly can harness that emotional power to make a change.

In the Shema, we are told to love Hashem "bechol levavecha", which literally translates as "with all your heart". The heart is the seat of all emotions. We are asked to love Hashem with all our emotions – both negative and positive. But how can we love Hashem with negative emotions?

The answer lies in the process of increasing our emotional intelligence. The Oxford English Dictionary defines emotional intelligence as "the capacity to be aware of, control, and express one's emotions, and to handle interpersonal relationships judiciously and empathetically". Research shows that people with high levels of emotional intelligence have greater career success (Cooper, 1997).

Without awareness, there cannot be control, as there is no way we can process an emotion that we do not even realise exists.

Awareness is the first step, and control is the second. Without awareness, there cannot be control, as there is no way we can process an emotion that we do not even realise exists.

As we learn to stop and think, we can check in with ourselves and assess which emotion is influencing our mind at this moment. It is not a question of denial or subjugation. Feelings need to be acknowledged, understood and then channelled into useful responses.

With direction and guidance, whatever emotion a person feels can be directed towards the service of Hashem, and thereby bring something positive to the world.

Onwards and Upwards

PARSHAT BEHA'ALOTECHA, JUNE 2018

Sometimes people ask me how my week was, and often I have to stop and think: what did I do this week?

The pace of life in the 21st century is fast and furious. We are inundated with information and kept busy throughout the day.

I wonder, though, if we are paying enough attention to consciously planning our day or whether we are just going through the motions.

There is a saying that life is like a downwards escalator; if we are not walking upwards, then we will be pulled down.

(This week I flew to Vienna and saw, first-hand, that it is a rather difficult task, when I tried to walk backwards on the airport escalator!)

Many of the things we do are important and I'm not suggesting that we totally change track. Sometimes, though, with a little bit of learning or thought, we can change our lives without changing our routine.

Our mindset affects how we view our lives. In the morning, it is good to make a plan for the day. However, it would help us to remember that 'Man plans and G-d laughs'. If we hand over those plans to Hashem, then we can let go of the results.

It would help us to remember that 'Man plans and G-d laughs'. If we hand over those plans to Hashem, then we can let go of the results.

We can take a look at our schedule and see where we can help someone else within that structure. Maybe we can offer a colleague to help them on a project or offer a compliment on a job well done.

If we are shopping, could we pick up something small that would bring a member of our family or a neighbour some joy?

There is a mitzva in the Torah to love Hashem (we read it in the Shema: "Ve'ahavta et Hashem Elokecha"). When we are stuck in traffic or waiting in a queue, we could just think of all the blessings in our life, thank Hashem for them and feel love for Hashem. Easy mitzva!

In Parshat Beha'alotecha, it talks about Aaron ascending the steps towards the Menorah. The first word is 'beha'alotecha', when you go up. It made me think: am I going up?

Life is so short, and the opportunities to elevate ourselves are many. We are so blessed to be able to modify our actions only slightly and thereby bring ourselves and the world to a better place.

A Real Court Case

THE SHABBAT BEFORE YOM KIPPUR, SEPTEMBER 2018

Let us set the scene. Right now, each one of us is sitting in a court room.

In this courtroom, there are no prosecutors or defenders. There are only our own actions. Acted out in front of us, with our thoughts and intentions clearly displayed.

It's not a question of arguing what is or is not the truth. G-d is Omniscient. Hashem knows the truth. Hashem knows our intentions and knows what we did in private. There is no escaping the reality of what we have or have not achieved over the last year.

Right now, it is being decided. Will we live? Or will we die? Will it be peaceful? Or stressful? By fire? Or by water? (as in the "Unetaneh Tokef" prayer in the Yom Kippur Prayer Book).

I can feel the shivers; my neck is tensing up. What have I done? What will be?

Yet we are told at the end of that prayer that Teshuva, Tefilla and Tzedaka (Repentance, Prayer and Charity) change the decree.

I always used to read that and think that was great. We're safe. We are given a free ticket out of that stressful place.

I am sorry and I'm praying and I'll give some charity and I'm done. The day is over and I can continue life as normal.

Teshuva, Tefilla and Tzedaka are indeed a magic formula, but they only work when we have sincerely worked on fulfilling them properly.

Actually, it's not so simple. Today, I sat quietly in a room and tried to do some proper teshuva. The act of repentance involves admitting the sin, regretting it sincerely, and committing toward the future. The problem is that I don't want to say aloud what I did wrong. It's really uncomfortable. I don't want to make myself think deeply about what I did and how it affected people around me. Teshuva is hard.

We tend to live our lives with a barrier around our hearts that enables us to function on a day-to-day basis. We do something wrong, and we move on. We forgive ourselves, and forget it happened. Now I must stop and think and relive that moment – those deeds that I buried deep inside. This is proper work.

Prayer, too, is not an easy task. I am not great at concentrating at the best of times. The minute I open the Siddur, my mind wanders: What shall I make for supper? When will I have time to return some clothes to the shop? Did I remember Basya's lunch? When, eventually, I remind myself that I am actually talking to Hashem, I try to concentrate once more. The words feel so distant....

So, why am I sharing this with you?

Because I believe that Hashem is a loving and kind G-d, who is patient and wants to bless us with a good year. Hashem waits for us to make the effort and rewards us for every attempt. Teshuva, Tefilla and Tzedaka are indeed a magic formula, but they only work when we have sincerely worked on fulfilling them properly.

We cannot simply turn up on Yom Kippur and expect that saying the words will repair the damage.

This is our last Shabbat before Yom Kippur. Our rabbis say, "Call G-d when He is close" (Isaiah 55:6). Right now, Hashem is so close, and we can use this time to try to prepare ourselves and do some true soul searching, so that together we can be ready to approach and enter Yom Kippur.

May you all be blessed with a happy, healthy and successful year.

An Eye That Sees

FEBRUARY 2019

A few weeks ago, the school where I work installed security cameras in all the classrooms. I work in a classroom and didn't know about this until one morning when I spotted a camera facing directly at me. It was disconcerting and made me feel quite uncomfortable. The knowledge that I was being recorded as I did my work, and ate my lunch, made me a little nervous.

In Ethics of Our Fathers 2:1, Rabbi Yehuda the Prince writes "Know what is above you: an eye that sees, and an ear that hears, and all your deeds are written in a book".

In Judaism, we believe that all physical experiences in this world mirror the spiritual reality. I felt this quite vividly that week.

Hashem also has 'security cameras', but they are much more sophisticated for two reasons:

1. *They are with us every day and night, and everywhere we go.*
2. *They don't only record our actions; they also record our thoughts, struggles and choices.*

This is a sobering thought and yet it can also be an empowering one. Hashem notices and records every time we overcome our urge to do wrong. Hashem sees our internal struggles and our inner triumphs. Holding ourselves back when we wanted to say something unkind, working on our thoughts to think positively about someone else's mistakes, and even planning to help someone but not managing to fulfil that plan – all these are recorded in our very own book of life. This book is signed by us, as we read in the High Holy Day prayers: "and each person's signature is in it".

> *Know what is above you: an eye that sees, and an ear that hears, and all your deeds are written in a book.*

When I met with the security team at school and voiced my concerns, they replied that it is uncomfortable at first, but most people just get used to it and forget after a while.

In the meantime, it is a great reminder to me to be careful with everything I do. Each thought, word and action is recorded in my book and I would really like to hope that it will be a pleasant book to read when it is complete.

Playing Our Own Tune

PESACH, APRIL 2019

We recently had the privilege of hearing a live orchestra at the Royal Festival Hall. It was fascinating to watch how a group of approximately 50 musicians walk into a room, pick up their instruments, and suddenly transform the room with the most beautiful music.

At one point in the concert, the violinists were all playing in sync, except for one, who was playing a different part. The violinist was not standing on his own; he was sitting right in the middle of all the other musicians.

As I watched him play his part, I was amazed how he managed to concentrate on his part without being confused by all the other notes around him. He was immersed in his music and had total focus on his own instrument.

It made me think about our lives as Jews, living in a world filled with

many other people. We are part of the world, and yet we have our own 'piece' to play. When Hashem took us out of Egypt, we became Hashem's nation. Forty-nine days later, Hashem gave us the Torah and there we formed a bond that cannot be broken.

Yet, we live in a world amongst all different religions and cultures – each one playing their own music – and it is not always so easy for us to remember who we are and our role in the world. We may become distracted by the sounds around us. We went down to Egypt as a family, but after two hundred years we were immersed in their culture and were almost lost. Hashem saved us, but in order to be rescued we needed to know who we were and that we wanted to be Hashem's people.

Every year, we re-live the experience of coming out of Egypt. We discuss what happened to us, and our miraculous redemption. It is true that the Seder is meant to remind us of our past, but its purpose is also to give us a strong mission for the future. Now that the Seder is behind us, perhaps it

The Seder is meant to remind us of our past, but its purpose is also to give us a strong mission for the future.

would be good to ask ourselves some of the following questions:

- *Am I aware of what it means to be a Jew?*
- *Do I have my own personal connection to Hashem?*
- *Do I get distracted by the music around me?*
- *How can I remain focused on fulfilling my unique mission?*

When each musician plays their own tune correctly, the harmonies blend together to fill this world with beautiful music.

May we merit to take the messages learnt from our Seder forward into our lives as strong, connected Jews, in this vast, diverse and multi-cultural world.

The Chosen People

SHAVUOT, JUNE 2019

Many Jews feel uncomfortable with the idea of being the 'chosen people'. It seems to imply superiority and a disdain for other nations of the world.

I'd like to look at the idea of being 'chosen' and what it means.

In the 17th century, Rabbi Moshe Chaim Luzzatto, in his great philosophical text "Derech Hashem" (Way of G-d), wrote that when Hashem created the world, it was done in order to give.

Hashem gave Adam and Eve, the first human beings, the opportunity to perfect the world (and receive the ultimate reward) by enjoying all the fruits of Eden and abstaining from just one tree. Unfortunately, they failed this test.

Hashem then opened up opportunities for many people to look and find G-d in this world. Abraham took those opportunities and chose Hashem in a world when monotheism was unheard of. He risked his life for Hashem and in return Hashem chose him as a faithful servant.

> *There is no greatness in being proud of our grandparents' choices; our lives are defined by the choices we make now.*

Isaac and Jacob perfected their own service of Hashem and their children were saved from Egypt on the merit of their keeping their faith, even under terribly difficult circumstances and in servitude.

Yet we did not truly become Hashem's people until Shavuot, the giving of the Torah. The Midrashic interpretation of the Sinai experience (Sifrei Devarim 343) explains that Hashem first gave all the other nations of the world an opportunity to accept the Torah, but they refused. Any nation could have become the Jewish people, but they chose not to accept the extra laws that the Torah requires.

When we made the decision to accept the Torah, some 3,000 years ago, we became the chosen nation. Yet, it was our choice. Now, living in the 21st century, it is our choice again. There is no greatness in being proud of our grandparents' choices; our lives are defined by the choices we make now.

Being a member of the Jewish people is a privilege and a responsibility. Our task is to be "a light unto the nations", to follow the laws of Hashem's Torah and thereby become a people worthy of Hashem's name.

We must respect all people (they are all made the image of G-d), deal justly in business and be true ambassadors of Hashem. Any individual who wishes to join our nation is able to do so, should they wish to choose to take on the extra requirements that becoming a Jew entails.

We do not believe that to perfect one's role in this world one needs to be Jewish. There are many 'righteous of the nations of the world' who have an exalted place in the world to come.

We are not a club; we are a mission. We chose Hashem and the Torah, and in return Hashem chose us, and promised to protect us even as we were scattered across the world.

This Shavuot, let us celebrate our chosen-ness by considering how we can ensure that our actions reflect the name of Hashem's people.

All Alone

ROSH HASHANA, SEPTEMBER 2019

Have you ever walked into a room full of people and felt all alone? Can you remember a time in school where you felt left out from the crowd?

There is a story in the Talmud about a man named Choni who slept for 70 years. He woke up to find that all his friends had died and a new generation had grown up in his town. Choni was devastated. He prayed for mercy and died. The Rabbis explain this episode as follows: "Ochevruta omituta" – either friendship or death!

We are social beings and we all crave friendship. In this fast-paced world, with social media and long work hours, studies have shown that we are more lonely than ever.

Sometimes, we can hurt another person's feelings without intending to. We become comfortable with our small group of friends and forget about a neighbour, a quieter classmate, or someone who lives a little further out.

It's not easy to find more time in the day, but even small gestures can make all the difference. A friendly call or text, going out for coffee, inviting someone to join you when you are going out anyway with a group of friends, or even inviting them for a Shabbat meal.

It may feel like a small effort on your part, but to someone else, it can mean the world!

If we could all decide to open up our hearts to a new friend, it could not only make a huge difference to that person, but it could serve to widen our perspectives on life too.

As a community, we try to be open and inclusive, and that is what makes Highgate so special. For this new year, can we take on the challenge of spreading that warmth just a little bit further?

Time to Come Home

SUCCOT, OCTOBER 2019

Two friends, Hannah and Claire, went to school together. They enjoyed each other's company and always looked out for one another. Once, Hannah was ill in hospital and Claire drove for over three hours to bring her some soup and keep her company.

Over the years, they drifted apart. Despite Claire's efforts to maintain their friendship, Hannah became busy with her own life and seemed to forget about her friend.

As Claire grew up, she missed Hannah and wanted to reconnect – but she wasn't sure if Hannah was interested.

Claire wrote her a long letter and awaited a response with nervous anticipation. After a few days, Hannah sent back a reply with a small package. In it was a pot of soup, wrapped up with words of reconciliation and an invitation to come and stay.

Claire was thrilled and relieved to see that her words were accepted, and that Hannah still wanted their friendship. The soup served as a reminder that Hannah hadn't forgotten Claire's kindness, and that their connection was real.

It's felt like a marathon over these past few weeks, with all the High Holidays. We have come to Shul and tried to reconnect with Hashem. We have apologised and prayed and hoped that our prayers have been accepted.

On Succot, we sit in the Succah and remember how Hashem sheltered and protected us all those years in the desert. And Hashem remembers how we trusted and followed Him into the desert with no idea of how we would survive.

We have rekindled our connection during the High Holidays and Hashem has forgiven us for drifting away from Him, so now we can enjoy that special relationship.

We have rekindled our connection during the High Holidays and Hashem has forgiven us for drifting away from Him, so now we can enjoy that special relationship.

It's not so easy being in a Succah in England in the rain and cold. (I highly recommend that you go to Israel for Succot if you ever have the opportunity. It is the most beautiful time of year there – and not just because of the weather!)

Not many people have a Succah at home, and you are all welcome to come to any of the services over Succot and take an opportunity to sit in the Succah and take a moment to feel Hashem's presence and love.

Even if you are all 'shul-ed out', you could find a friend's Succah to make a blessing in, or perhaps just sit in your garden (with an umbrella!) and take a few moments to remember that Hashem is with you always, everywhere.

Whichever way you choose to connect to the Chag, I wish you all a beautiful, joyous Succot.

The Other Side of the Story

DECEMBER 2019

This morning, I was waiting in the queue at the local post office. In front of me was a mother with three children: twin girls and an older brother. They were all between about nine and ten years old.

Understandably, they were a little bored and were playing around with each other. The mother was facing the front of the queue and every so often turned around and told them to behave. Specifically, she was scolding the older boy and asking him to stop bothering the girls.

We judge ourselves by our intentions, but judge others by their actions.

As I was behind them, I could see what was really going on. The girls were annoying their older brother, pinching his cheeks, and smacking his back. He was responding to their provocation, but when the mother turned around, she only saw his response. By the time they left the post office, the mother was exasperated and told the older brother that he was in big trouble when they got home. I felt so bad for him.

One of the commandments in the Torah is "B'tzedek tishpot amitecha" - You shall judge your fellow with righteousness (Leviticus 19:15). When we judge a person, we are not always aware of the whole story. So it is very important to try to find a positive slant to their actions, or at least spend some time trying to find out the full story.

Sometimes we fall into a pattern of judging people negatively because of past behaviour or our own insecurities. Practising looking for the good takes time and energy, but not only will we be then fulfilling Hashem's instructions, we will also find ourselves in a more positive space.

I once read a book called "The Other Side of the Story" by Yehudis Samet. It is full of real-life scenarios when someone was judged for their actions, but the truth was so different from what seemed to be reality. We can never truly know or understand the thought process of another, and we are often not privy to all the background information.

Steven Covey, the late American educator, author and businessman, wrote in his best-selling book, "The Speed of Trust": "We judge ourselves by our intentions, but judge others by their actions".

This way of thinking has caused many arguments and much sadness in the world.

Let us try to look for the good inside all those we meet and judge them favourably.

Home Visit

MARCH 2020

(This post took place during the lockdown caused by the Covid-19 pandemic. I wanted to include it in this book as it helps me appreciate the gift of an open Shul and being allowed to go out of our home whenever we like.)

This morning, I went into Shul to daven. I loved the quiet, coming from a house full of people in lock- down. Yet somehow, it was lonely. It made me think of our community – and how much I miss you all.

I hope you are well, and coping with these difficult times. For those of you who are ill, my thoughts are with you and we all pray for your recovery.

I just wanted to share a small thought.

Shul is a place we come to 'visit' and connect with Hashem. Especially on Shabbat, we feel the holiness of the day by coming to Shul and davening together. At the moment, we cannot be there, and we need to create that special Shabbat experience at home.

Home is a place where we bring Hashem into our lives. How can we do that?

We are taught that angels come and visit us in our home on Friday night. We can welcome them by creating an atmosphere that is conducive for a connection to Hashem. Anything we do to make Shabbat special is a mitzva: the mitzva of honouring Shabbat. We can lay a nice white tablecloth on our table, put on some lovely clothes, light the candles, and have some nice food and a glass of wine. We can sing some Shabbat songs and talk to Hashem in our own words.

> *Shul is a place we come to 'visit' and connect with Hashem...*
>
> *Home is a place where we bring Hashem into our lives.*

There is a lot of anxiety about our current situation, and the media does a spectacular job of streaming information our way. The problem is that the more we read, the more anxious we become. Dr Yehuda Yifrach writes that anxiety and depression reduce the power of the body to deal with pathological threats and to heal itself.

In a way, because we are at home together all week, it can be difficult to feel special on Shabbat. Yet, there is one thing we can do, which will be good for our bodies and our souls. Let's try to turn off our phones and give the media a break.

We can focus inwards and go for a walk (when allowed*) without the constant updates. We can enjoy looking around at the beautiful blossoms and the lovely sunshine.

Wishing you a peaceful and spiritually connected Shabbat.

---

* At the time of writing, Government guidelines allowed a person to leave their home once a day for some exercise.

What Will Be Tomorrow?

PARSHAT BEHAR, MAY 2020

This week, our Prime Minister gave us an update on the Government's plans for fighting the coronavirus. Although he tried to be hopeful, we were left with many questions and uncertainties about the future.

Many of us are, understandably, anxious and worry about the future. Parsha Behar gives us an idea about how to deal with these worries. The parsha talks about the mitzva of 'Shmitta', the mitzva to leave the land to rest for one year in every seven years. This was basically asking all farmers (in the land of Israel) to give up their livelihood for one whole year and trust that Hashem that will provide. Quite a big ask!

Hashem knows our nature and addresses the question that a farmer will inevitably ask. "And should you ask: 'What will we eat in the seventh year, if we may neither sow nor gather in our crops?' I will ordain my blessings for you in the sixth year and it will yield a crop sufficient for three years" (Leviticus 25:18–21).

I often find that the fear of a future possible event is worse than the event itself. In the example of the Shmitta, although we are told that there would be enough produce to last for the seventh year, it's difficult for a farmer not to worry. This worry could eclipse the enjoyment of produce over the preceding six years. Of course, we need to plan as best we can for the following years, but the results are in Hashem's hands.

We are not currently equipped to deal with tomorrow's problems, because Hashem only gives us the tools and the strength to deal with a challenge at the time when we are experiencing it.

We are not currently equipped to deal with tomorrow's problems, because Hashem only gives us the tools and the strength to deal with a challenge at the time when we are experiencing it. Hashem does not give those tools in advance, and therefore the worry is painful and futile.

In our lives, we are confronted with so much tragedy. It is hard to remain positive and see the blessings that exist in front of us now, when there is fear of what the future holds. Yet, there are positive moments, and those need to be noticed and valued.

I was recently talking to a friend who mentioned that she feels a little guilty to feel joy at such a difficult time. I do too.

There is a time to cry (during prayer – every heartfelt prayer is precious) and a time to be happy. Noticing the good does not mean devaluing another person's pain. It is an internal feeling that can infuse those around us with positivity and hope.

When we have trust in Hashem, we can be grateful for the blessings of today, without allowing the cloud of worry about tomorrow to block out that joyous moment. The thoughts could vary in severity: 'Today, the sun is shining – yes; but tomorrow it might rain', or 'I have enough money to last for this week, but what will be when that money runs out?' or even worse "I am well today, but what happens if I'm not well tomorrow?"

All these worries flow through our mind, and it is a pity to let them rob us of the pleasure of the gifts we have at this very moment. It is not easy to push those worries away, and it will take time for us to change the reflex reaction of worry that appears in our brain immediately after a positive thought occurs, especially during challenging times.

Through working on increasing our trust in Hashem, we can learn to treasure each happy moment, and ensure that our worries for tomorrow will not eclipse the joy of today.

Unmuted

MAY 2020

> *"Integrity is doing the right thing,*
> *even when no one else is watching.*
>
> C.S. Lewis

Have you ever un-muted yourself on a conference call without realising it? We had that experience at a recent online Kabbalat Shabbat service and, although it was really embarrassing, we were so grateful that we didn't say anything too terrible (I hope!).

It made me think about life during lockdown. On the one hand, we were at home all day and therefore we could 'let our guard down' and just be ourselves. But on the other hand, when we joined a Zoom call, we could be exposing ourselves to a large number of people without even realising it.

Most people dress better, behave better and talk better when they are in public. However, it is at home where we truly see who we are. During lockdown, when we were at home so much of the time, it was hard to have patience and love for those who were around us constantly (including ourselves).

The Book of Numbers, Bamidbar, deals with the Jewish journey in the wilderness. It talks of arguments and complaints, and the regular mundane activities of the Jews at that time. Unlike the other books of the Torah, it contains no momentous events and yet it is included in our five books. This is when we became a people.

Sometimes, it is easier to rise to the occasion when something huge hits. The day-to-day arguments and difficulties may not feel like worthwhile challenges to overcome. The Book of Numbers teaches us that we developed as a people through these small daily challenges, in the privacy of our own homes.

Although lockdown was very challenging for us, and many suffered great personal losses, we also faced every day at home with small tests too. Those small tests can help to define our character.

When no one else is looking, the test becomes harder. What difference does it make anyway?

Most people dress better, behave better and talk better when they are in public. However, it is at home where we truly see who we are.

In Judaism, we believe that Hashem is with us always, and notices and rewards every tiny act or choice. As the American psychologist Wayne Dyer said, "Our life is the sum total of each choice we made". Without the help of peer pressure, we need to strengthen our inner resolve to do the right thing – even when no one else sees.

Children's Prayer

MAY 2020

There is a special prayer that we say on the day before the new month of Sivan and six days before Shavuot, the festival marking the giving of the Torah.

The words of the prayer were written by the Shelah, Rav Yeshayahu ben Avraham Horowitz (1555–1630), on children's education. They are requests that mothers and fathers have made of Hashem, generation after generation.

This year, parenting has been more challenging than ever. Rather than sending our children off to school, with a hug and a kiss, and then going to work, we are teaching them at home. They are with us all day, every day, and watching and learning from our behaviour. It is stressful if one has work too, and there are so many balls to juggle.

We have had to adjust our goals and accept that learning comes in many different forms. We are learning to get along with one another. We are learning to have patience and lower expectations. Hopefully, we are also learning to have some fun with our children too, so that when this stage passes (soon I hope!), we will have some positive memories of the time we all spent together.

As our kids return slowly to school, we parents have also learned that we are their most important educators, and our prayers for them are the most powerful education tool we have.

HERE IS ONE SEGMENT OF THE SHELAH'S PRAYER:

May we, our offspring, and the offspring of all Your people, the House of Israel, know Your Name and study Your Torah. . . and grant Your children health, honour, strength, and give them stature, beauty, charm and kindness, and may there be love, brotherhood and peace among them, and may they serve you with love and with reverence... that they should be only peaceful and truthful and good and straight in the eyes of Hashem and in the eyes of all human beings.

If you are not blessed with children, you can pray for any child you know. Every prayer counts. May Hashem answer all our prayers and grant us children who follow in Hashem's ways.

The Positive Side of Jealousy

MAY 2020

We've all been told how harmful jealousy is for us. It is so high up on the list of bad traits that it is included in the Ten Commandments.

"Jealousy rots the bones" says King Solomon, in his book of Proverbs (14:30).

However, there are times when jealousy can actually be useful – when it spurs us on to achieve more. If we are jealous of another's success and it inspires us to work hard to accomplish our own goals, then that jealousy is sacred.

The Talmud (Bava Batra 21a) teaches that "kinat sofrim tarbeh chochmah" – the [proper] envy of scholars stimulates more learning.

My dear husband is a great person. When he sets his mind to something, he works tirelessly to achieve his goal. A couple of years ago, he decided to improve his health by starting to run. We bought a running machine, and he worked each week consistently. I was quite jealous of his success, and this encouraged me to try to do the same.

For this Shavuot, he had set himself an even more important goal: finishing the entire Shas (2711 pages of the Talmud). Day in, day out, he completed one page at a time and 7.5 years later, we are celebrating together. I, too, wanted to feel like I can complete something, so I started my own daily learning schedule of less than 5 minutes a day, to learn all the 613 mitzvot (commandments) of the Torah. It is not comparable to what he achieved, but it is manageable with my current schedule.

If we are jealous of another's success and it inspires us to work hard to accomplish our own goals, then that jealousy is sacred.

When we see a person accomplish something worthwhile, we may feel that they are greater than us and we could never achieve such a goal. Instead of thinking this way, perhaps we can allow ourselves to be inspired by the greatness we see and use that envy to motivate ourselves to grow in our own way, through manageable small steps.

Infectious Yawning

JUNE 2020

Have you ever noticed that when someone yawns near you, you end up yawning yourself?

Yawns are quite infectious and, despite the fact that the other person had no intention of influencing your breathing behaviour, the sight of the yawn elicits a reaction inside you and the yawn just appears.

It is fascinating to note how we can influence one another with our actions, without realising it at all.

Often, we come across other people's negative traits and that can infuriate us. Seeing someone behave badly grates on our nerves and we may wish that we could somehow change them to stop that behaviour. The Talmud (Kiddushim 70a) writes "Shmuel says: If one habitually claims that others are flawed, he disqualifies himself with his own flaw." The flaw one accuses others of having is, in fact, the one that he has.

It is so easy to see what others are doing wrong, but harder to look inside oneself and recognise our own flaws. When we see a behaviour that bothers us, it is good to look inwards and check when we may display that same character flaw. This way, we can improve ourselves – which will ultimately change our environment too.

When we see a behaviour that bothers us, it is good to look inwards and check when we may display that same character flaw.

For example, if we are frustrated that a friend is constantly interrupting us during a conversation, then it would be a great idea to study our own behaviour with others. We may notice that we are doing the same thing ourselves. Or as Winston Churchill put it so eloquently, "Will you please stop interrupting me when I am interrupting you!"

We are often so quick to see others' faults and our initial reaction is to judge them, but perhaps we can use those discoveries to help us work on ourselves instead. This way, like with our infectious yawns, we can begin to "Be the change that you wish to see in the world" (Mahatma Gandhi).

The Power to Bless

JUNE 2020

This week, a colleague left a lovely message for me on the phone. It was full of blessings and I felt those blessings wash over me and bring light to my day. Every time I think of the message, I feel grateful and encouraged to continue the work I do.

Words spoken might seem to vanish into thin air, but their effect on us can last a lifetime.

Try to think back to a comment that affected you. Whether it was positive or negative – the words can still be heard in your mind, and most probably the speaker does not even remember saying them.

There is a beautiful custom on Friday night for parents to bless one's children. The text of that blessing, reads as follows:

"May G-d bless you and guard you. May G-d's face shine on you, and find favour in you. May G-d's face lift toward you and give you peace" (Numbers 6:24–26).

This blessing has been given by the priests for over 2,000 years, and we continue to hear those blessings in Shul throughout the year (and in Israel, they bless the people every day).

Rabbi Hanina said in the Talmud (Megilla 15a):

"One should never regard the blessing of an ordinary person as light (unimportant) in your eyes, since two of the great men of their generations received blessings from ordinary people and those blessings were fulfilled in them. And they were David and Daniel. David, for Arau-

Words spoken might seem to vanish into thin air, but their effect on us can last a lifetime.

nah blessed him, as it is written: 'And Araunah said to the king, May the Lord your God accept you' (II Samuel 24:23), and it was fulfilled. Daniel, for Darius blessed him, as it is written: 'Your God Whom you serve continually, He will rescue you' (Daniel 6:17), and this too was fulfilled when Daniel was saved from the lions' den.

Sometimes, we may feel like our words are not so powerful, because we are just ordinary people, but the Talmud teaches us that we have more power than we realise.

At this moment in world history, there is so much pain, anger and sadness. Let us use the power of our mouths to give blessings to those around us and bring joy and hope to all that we meet.

Am I Willing?

JULY 2020

There are times in our life when we are asked to do something out of our comfort zone. The first question we might ask ourselves is "Am I able? Is this something that I have the skills to accomplish?" This seems a totally reasonable response to the question.

However, if we look over at great people's lives, we will find that they accomplished more than they ever thought possible. Different situations can bring out potential in a person that they never realised they possessed.

An American professor and motivational speaker, Charlie Harary, once had the opportunity to have a chat with a high-ranking Israeli officer in the Secret Service. Harary tried to ask some questions about the officer's bravery and how he must have always wanted to be in the army. The officer replied that this was not his intention at all when he was young.

Unfortunately, his father was injured whilst fighting for his country when he was 11 years old. Together with his mother and family, he tried to care for him and help him recover, One day, his father called him into his bedroom and said to him, "It's time for you to be a man". He was frightened and worried and replied "But I'm just a boy. I am not able to".

His father was not a religious man, but he knew the Torah. "You think Avraham was ready? You think Yosef was ready? What about Moshe and

Dovid? Do you think people are ready when the time comes for them? You don't have to be able or ready; you just have to be willing."

And with that, the intelligence officer concluded, "Every day I am in the army, I think that even if I can't, if I try, G-d will give me the strength to do the things I think I can't do."

In life, when you are willing to try to do something you think you can't do, Hashem can help you get there. Even if you don't know how it will work out, you can accomplish something, as long as you are willing.

> *Each human being is capable of achieving great things if they are willing to venture out of their own little bubble, and trust that Hashem will help them.*

When Moshe was asked to lead the Jewish people, he replied, "I am not a man of words" and "I am heavy of mouth and heavy of tongue" (Exodus 4:10). Yet the book of Deuteronomy is one very long speech given by Moshe, who led the Jewish people for over 40 years. Quite an amazing feat for one who is "not a man of words"! This speech has been learnt by millions of people across the world. Moshe achieved more than he could ever have dreamed of.

Each human being is capable of achieving great things if they are willing to venture out of their own little bubble, and trust that Hashem will help them. It is a little scary, but the results might just surprise you.

Reaching the Roots

JULY 2020

The other day, I wanted to have a break from my various jobs and decided to do some gardening. I find gardening very therapeutic; it keeps my hands busy, my head focused, and I can enjoy the fresh scents of plants and flowers around me.

My least favourite part is weeding. My father told me that the best way to remove weeds is by pulling them out by their roots. When I have the energy and the right tools, I follow his advice. On other days, I just remove the weeds at the ground, which inevitably leads to them regrowing rather quickly.

Our rabbis say that when a person wants to fix a negative character trait, they need to look at the root of the problem. Stopping the behaviour may seem to fix the sin, but unless we deal with the cause, we won't succeed.

Stopping the behaviour may seem to fix the sin, but unless we deal with the cause, we won't succeed.

For example, if somebody's usual response to an unkind comment is to lash out with an angry response, then a good solution would seem to be to learn to keep quiet instead. However, keeping quiet might not erase the pain inside. Simply holding back may mean that the hatred is felt within, as it says, "You shall not harbour hatred towards your brother in your heart" (Leviticus 19:17). Or even worse, that anger could be inadvertently taken out upon someone else.

Dealing with the root of a problem means looking inside ourselves and becoming aware of what we are feeling. We can then try to deal with that emotion, rather than trying to squash it down and have it 'pop up' elsewhere.

We don't like to admit to ourselves that we have negative emotions, but we are all human, and the first step for real lasting change is awareness. From this place, we can compassionately help ourselves to see the situation differently. Perhaps the original comment was misunderstood or maybe the speaker was having a hard day. It could even be that the comment was not directed at us at all! When we accept and recognise our emotions, we can then ask Hashem to help us respond in the correct way.

It is more work to dig deep and find the root of our actions, rather than just deal with what is on the surface but, as with gardening, the results are longer lasting.

Wishing you a wonderful week of successful spiritual gardening.

A Time to Yearn

SHIVA ASAR B'TAMUZ, JULY 2020

This Shabbat is so exciting for us as we re-open the Shul and welcome back our community. Yet it is still with a heavy heart, as we remember all those people we have lost due to this terrible pandemic.

During this time, when the Shul was closed, I felt a sense of sadness and longing for all the people, the noise, the camaraderie and the friendship that we are blessed with every week. Each week, we get to hear our members' news, the good and the bad, as we share our lives together and hopefully also find time to pray and connect with Hashem too!

This week, we will need to try to do this through masks and with social distancing. No singing and no hugs. Although it will be great to see you, there is still something that will be missing in our Shul – our home. We are one step closer, but the yearning for true closeness remains.

On Thursday, we fasted to commemorate the beginning of the destruction of our Temple, our Bet Hamikdash. Thus begins the three weeks of mourning for what we lost over 2,000 years ago.

I have always found it difficult to mourn something that I never saw or experienced. Coupled with the fact that the summer holidays are coming up, it is hard to dampen one's mood to think of the great loss to our people.

This year though, in a small way, I can relate to that sense of yearning. Our Shul looked sad and forlorn, the

Hashem wants to bring us home, to Jerusalem. Yet Hashem can only do so when we truly want to come.

walls casting a dark shadow over its empty pews. Whilst the Bet Hamikdash has not yet been rebuilt, a Shul holds some of the Temple's precious sanctity. At times, I sat in Shul on my own and thought about the sadness of a parent who longs to see their children. I cried for Hashem and I cried for us.

The Talmud states that "All who mourn [the destruction of] Jerusalem will merit to see it in its joy" (Ta'anit 30b). The sadness that we are supposed to feel during this period of time is not merely to mourn the bitter past, but to long for a better future.

Perhaps this year, we can use our current life experience to help us feel this sense of yearning. Hashem wants to bring us home, to Jerusalem. Yet Hashem can only do so when we truly want to come.

Hashem is hidden in this world, and many deny Hashem's very existence. Let us feel the pain of a parent who is continuously giving and is yet mostly unnoticed. Let us hope together for a time where the world will unite in recognition of Hashem and live together in kindness and justice.

May we merit together to see Jerusalem in its joy.

Why Are We Still Crying?

TISHA B'AV, JULY 2020

Today is Tisha B'av and we are still crying about an event that took place 2000 years ago. What really happened and what does it have to do with us now?

The Second Temple was physically destroyed by the Romans (in the year 70 CE), but our Sages explain that the main cause of its destruction was "baseless hatred".

Our rabbis say that each generation has the potential to rebuild the Temple.

You may be familiar with the story of Kamtza and Bar Kamtza. A man threw a huge party and invited all his friends. He asked his servant to invite his good friend, Kamtza, but the servant made a mistake and invited his enemy, Bar Kamtza, instead.

When the host saw his enemy enjoying the party, he was enraged and told him to leave. Bar Kamtza begged to be allowed to stay as he was embarrassed to leave – he even offered to pay for half of the party – but the host had no pity and threw him out. Bar Kamtza was so upset about this that he went to the Caesar and told him that the Jews were rebelling.

As a proof, he told the Caesar to send an animal to the Temple to offer as a sacrifice and explained that the Jews would refuse to offer it up. Caesar sent an animal that was perfect for a sacrifice, but Bar Kamtza made a small blemish on the animal, which meant that it was now not a kosher sacrifice. The Jews did not offer the animal, and the Caesar then decreed that the Temple should be destroyed.

One man. One party. Many guests. No one stood up for Bar Kamtza. He was humiliated and, thousands of years later, we are still suffering the consequences.

But that isn't our fault – it's theirs! So why are we still mourning?

Our rabbis say that each generation has the potential to rebuild the Temple. It was destroyed because of baseless hatred, and it can be rebuilt with baseless love. If it hasn't been built in our days, then we haven't yet learnt the lesson of baseless love. Loving another and being kind to one another just because.

Today, together, we can make a difference by adding some love and kindness to our day. Maybe there is someone we are still angry with about a past misdeed, or perhaps we may have hurt someone else with our words. Now is a great time to make that call, write that letter or even go and visit.

We can all do something, however small, and we hope and pray that this will be the end of our mourning and the beginning of our redemption.

When Things Go Wrong

AUGUST 2020

Some days everything goes according to plan and we sail through the day. Most days, however, something goes wrong. Maybe a flat tyre, a lost shoe, a parking ticket, or frustration with the bank.

It's easy to thank Hashem when things go our way, but much harder when we encounter setbacks and difficulties.

Our rabbis teach us "Just as we thank Hashem for the good, so we should thank Hashem for the bad" (Talmud Brachot 54a). That is an extremely difficult thing to do. We have our plans and our goals for the day and are naturally disappointed when faced with problems along the way. How can we thank Hashem for them?

The first of our 13 Principles of Faith is "I believe with complete faith that the Creator, blessed be G-d's name, is the Creator and Guide for all created beings. G-d alone made, makes and will make all that is created."

Hashem loves us and everything Hashem does is for our good, even when we cannot see it. The more we internalise this concept, the happier lives we will lead. There are so many elements of life that are not within our control, and it is so much more painful to feel 'unlucky' rather than know it may be uncomfortable but it is for the best, and designed exclusively for me.

A couple of nights ago, my sister and her family were invited to a friend's triplet sons' bar mitzva party, an hour away from her home. They were only able to leave home late and every traffic light they encountered was red. It was extremely frustrating as they wanted to make sure to be able to be there before the simcha ended, so they could wish the family 'mazel tov'. After a while of stressing about the red lights, my sister reminded the family that we should thank Hashem for what goes wrong.

> *It's easy to thank Hashem when things go our way, but much harder when we encounter setbacks and difficulties.*

So, they all thanked Hashem for the next couple of red lights. The rest of the journey, the lights were all green!

Obviously, this is unlikely to happen with everyone's problems, but it was a lovely reminder that Hashem runs the world, and if we truly thank and trust Hashem, our lives will be much richer.

May Hashem bless you all, and may we merit to see Hashem's goodness clearly.

P.S. This article was written to help us with the regular daily challenges in life, such as red lights. Real tragedies, illness and loss of a loved one are obviously much more difficult to cope with and need further study. I highly recommend a book called "Why Bad Things Don't Happen to Good People", written by Rabbi Shaul Rosenblatt after his wife died of cancer, leaving him with four young children.

Why Didn't You Answer My Prayers?

AUGUST 2020

When it comes to things like bad traffic, missed trains or lost cards, the experiences are annoying or irritating but not devastating. Thanking Hashem for those minor difficulties in life is difficult, but possible.

Yet, there are some situations that are so much more painful, such as serious illness or the loss of a loved one. In these situations, there are no easy fixes or happy solutions. Living with them can be emotionally exhausting and unbearable. We may pray for recovery, but it seems that our prayers are not answered.

When I was young, my sister's father-in-law was ill with cancer. He was 56 years old, and we all davened very sincerely for his recovery. The doctors were not hopeful, but we knew that every prayer is powerful and many people in the community prayed for him daily.

I was in university at the time and was told that his situation had deteriorated. That day, I prayed with all my heart during the afternoon service and on the way home I prayed some more. When I arrived home, my parents informed me that he had passed away that morning.

I was devastated. So many prayers. So many tears. Where did they all go? Were they in vain?

He was so young, and he left behind a wife and seven children. I had truly believed that our prayers would help him recover.

For a while, I lost my connection to prayer and felt lost with my faith. Does Hashem really listen anyway?

I asked these questions to a family friend, who gave me the following response:

"We cannot comprehend Hashem's ways, and they are always just and right. Each person lives for the amount of time that was correct for them.

Every prayer is indeed powerful and has some effect on the world – although it may not be the one that we were hoping for. The doctors had given this man six weeks to live, and he lived for another two and a half years. Who knows if those prayers gave him a few more days or even minutes of life?

Every heartfelt prayer changes this world, brings us connection to the Creator, and opens up the heavenly channels of blessings, even if we cannot see it.

His family needed support during this difficult time, and the prayers may help them receive the support they need for the coming years. Those prayers also accompany this man on his journey to the Next World and help bring him merit there."

I found comfort in my friend's words, and I'm sharing them with you now, for perhaps they may give comfort for those of you who have been through a difficult time recently.

It is encouraging to hear when someone's prayers were 'successful', yet we all need Chizuk (strengthening) for those moments in life where it seems that we have not been heard.

As Rosh Hashana approaches, our prayers will be very different from other years. Some of you may not be able to come to shul and pray together with the community. The lack of atmosphere at home might make it difficult to connect to Hashem during prayers.

Let us try to strengthen ourselves and remember that every heartfelt prayer changes this world, brings us connection to the Creator, and opens up the heavenly channels of blessings, even if we cannot see it.

"May Hashem wipe away all the tears from all the land."

How to Connect when Feeling Disconnected,

ROSH HASHANA, SEPTEMBER 2020

This year, Rosh Hashana will be so different, and I can't even imagine how Shul will look without the throngs of people coming to celebrate the world's birthday together.

Actually, Rosh Hashana is the date that Adam and Eve were created. The world was created in the five days preceding Rosh Hashana, and its purpose is to house human beings, so that we can work hard to utilise it, preserve it and find Hashem in it (who hides behind nature).

It was only when humans arrived on the scene that the world's purpose could be fulfilled and Rosh Hashana is a day when we reflect on how well we are achieving that goal. We usually do this together in Shul, by singing songs of praise, thanking Hashem for all the good we have received in the past year, and praying for the coming year.

This year, many will be celebrating alone at home (and may not feel like celebrating at all). How can we reconnect spiritually without the uplifting tunes and the community feeling that embraces us as we step into a packed and vibrant Shul?

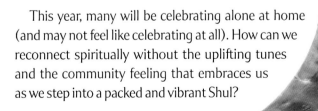

HERE ARE A FEW TIPS (SHARED BY SOME FRIENDS)

1. *One friend told me that they intend to walk to Shul on yom tov and stand nearby – they don't feel able to enter Shul at the moment but still want to feel connected. I thought it was an important lesson on how the little things matter, and how to try and adapt to the times.*

2. *Find and feel the holiness within you. You are a creation of Hashem, and there is a spark of holiness with you. Often that spark is awakened by listening to others. This year, Hashem wants us to find it within ourselves.*

3. *If you can, buy a book (or read or listen to a class online) about the High Holy Days and take some time to read and study in advance. Listen online to the tunes of the prayers (before Yom Tov) to reawaken those feelings of connection. Music touches the soul.*

4. *The theme of the High Holy Days is Teshuva, Tefilla and Tzedaka. Making these concepts practical to our situation right now, we can look to try to fulfil each of them on the day (or before):*

TESHUVA – REFLECT AND RETURN

It's been a hard year. Who have I become? A better or worse person? What parts of the 'lockdown me' do I want to keep, and which ones do I want to remove and start again? Take the time to look over the last year and do a helpful appraisal of your successes and failures. Don't get stuck in the guilt – that never helps! Only look back for the purpose of planning ahead.

TEFILLA – PRAYER

It's hard to pray alone. Sing loudly. Sing your own words. Maybe even dance? And if you are feeling sad, cry freely.

In Shul, we conform, and the unity is beautiful. At home, we need to find other ways to find and express our connection.

Ask Hashem for help. Hashem knows that it is hard to connect without the atmosphere. (At the beginning of the Amida silent prayer every day, we say "Hashem, open my lips". We need G-d's help even to be able to open our mouths!)

Hashem loves each one of us unconditionally. Hashem wants the best for us, and wants to grant us a year full of blessings. The blessings are there, but we need to unlock the channels, by asking and by thanking. There is no point showering blessings upon a person who doesn't notice them or appreciate them. Thank Hashem for the good you have received and beg with all your heart for more.

Many have been through so much pain that they cannot see any blessings. We can ask Hashem for help and support. Hashem listens to our tears and "supports the falling" (Morning Blessings, page 18 in the 'Green Siddur'). Tears are especially powerful if we direct them upwards into prayer.

TZEDAKA – CHARITY

Charity is not just about giving money. Giving can be done with one's presence and one's time. Now, more than ever, we appreciate the value of company. Visit someone or give them a call. This form of Chesed can be more meaningful than money. (Yet many are struggling financially – so if you do have the means, do open up your hearts and give to the many worthy causes around us. Hashem promises to refill those who share their wealth with those in need.)

Taking the time to work on all three of these themes, I really hope that we will be able to find connection in these difficult, disconnected times.

Wishing you a beautiful, meaningful and spiritually connected Yom Tov.

Out of Control

YOM KIPPUR, SEPTEMBER 2020

Right now, we are living in a world full of turmoil. Things seem to be spiralling out of control, the Covid-19 infection rate is rising, America seems to be falling apart, the economy is in dire straits, and we sit in our homes worrying what will be.

SO, HOW DO WE HANDLE THIS LACK OF CONTROL? THERE ARE A FEW DIFFERENT OPTIONS.

1. Live in a state of permanent anxiety: watch the news constantly, stockpile necessities and lock the doors.

2. Blame the authorities: "If it wasn't for China…", "It's all Trump's fault…", "Our government acted too late…".

3. Try to ignore reality and live as normal: ignore government health warnings and endanger the whole society.

The way Judaism looks at life, we have another option. Our rabbis tell us that everything that happens in the world is meant to teach us something, and we should learn from it and try to improve our ways. Each individual in this world is responsible for its state as a whole. We need to look at what is within our control and work our hardest to do what is right within.

We are not fooling anyone by behaving better; we are reaching into our true selves and allowing our innate goodness to shine.

On Yom Kippur, it is customary to take upon ourselves a commitment to improve in one area, to help us have a favourable judgement, in which Hashem grants us a year full of good health and success.

I always wondered about this custom. What is the point? Who are we kidding? It feels like when a headteacher turns up to a classroom and everyone suddenly behaves beautifully. The headteacher is pleased. But when she walks out of the classroom, everyone starts talking again. Was anything achieved?

The truth is that, deep down, we all want to improve and become greater people. We want to know that our lives are meaningful and to build our own spiritual connection to Hashem. Yet, life happens, and we are distracted by the various duties and work that we need to attend to.

The High Holy Days are opportunities for us to reflect and make a small change that will help us reach our true goal. We are not fooling anyone by behaving better; we are reaching into our true selves and allowing our innate goodness to shine.

A woman once asked her rabbi what improvement she should take upon herself. The rabbi told her to choose something small so that she will be able to continue the improvement throughout the year, rather than aim high and fail within a few weeks. The woman thought about it and returned with a small change. The Rabbi told her to take that change and cut it into half. (We often overestimate.)

The Torah is our guidebook for life, and there are many different mitzvot that we could choose to make a small improvement.

THE MITZVOT ARE SPLIT INTO TWO CATEGORIES:

1. **'Bein adam lechavero'** – Mitzvot between fellow people, for example loving one another, giving charity and being honest in business.

2. **'Bein adam leMakom'** – Mitzvot between people and Hashem, for example keeping Shabbat (buying special treats for Shabbat), keeping kosher (trying to go to a kosher butcher or bakery) and prayer (maybe say a small prayer each day – and you don't have to pray in Hebrew; English is also good!).

When choosing an area to improve, it is easier to choose something interpersonal, as those mitzvot make sense to us. We can see how these actions will affect the world. It is harder to work on the mitzvot that are more spiritual and less readily understandable.

When we choose to reach out of our comfort zone and try a new mitzva, it brings us close to Hashem, as it shows that we trust in Hashem and will try to follow Hashem's laws, even when we don't understand them and can't see their positive outcome.

Whichever path you choose, any improvement is worthwhile and will have a positive effect on the troubled world that we find ourselves in, as we start the new year.

Wishing you an easy fast, and meaningful Yom Kippur.

May Hashem bless you all with a year of growth and success and most importantly good health.

How Does It Work?

SIMCHAT TORAH, OCTOBER 2020

When we moved into our newly renovated home, it was incredibly exciting for all of us! The walls were freshly painted, the carpet was fresh and clean, and we were blessed with a beautiful new kitchen with all new equipment, and most importantly a Shabbat-compliant oven.

The only problem was that we needed to find the instructions. Without them, the oven stayed beautiful and clean, but a little bit useless. All those special buttons, but no idea what they did. We searched through the various papers amongst the packing boxes and we were delighted when the instruction booklet was found.

After reading them once, we worked out the basic instructions on how to use the oven, and then returned the booklet to the messy pile of papers strewn across the busy kitchen. The oven actually has many more options of different ways to cook and bake, but only if I take the time to read through those instructions again will I ever improve my culinary skills (rather than continually burning things – because I forgot about them in the oven!).

Soon, we will celebrate Simchat Torah. The day we finish reading the Torah and start reading it all over again. On this day, we sing and we dance with the Torah. Why?

> *The Torah is our life's instruction book, the best gift we could ever have asked for. Yet, it is often left sitting on the shelf.*

The Torah is our life's instruction book, the best gift we could ever have asked for. Yet, it is often left sitting on the shelf. Life could be more, if we only take the time to read it. Many of us have read the Torah on a surface level, so it may be difficult to see how those words guide us. But just like a medical journal, although it may seem unintelligible at first glance, the longer one studies it, the more wisdom one will find within it.

Hashem gave us this gift, and when we ignore its instructions it pains Hashem. Not for Hashem's own sake, but for ours. Imagine watching someone in an escape room. You can see their mistakes, and know the right answers, but you need to leave them to play – you cannot tell them the answers. Hashem gives us free choice and a book of instructions. Hashem wants the best for us and therefore guides us as much as possible, whilst still allowing us to choose our own path. We may not understand all of them (just as we don't always understand a doctor's medical advice), but if we follow them, we will see blessings.

If you can come to Shul, then please do make the effort to pop in – to see the Torah and thank Hashem for this gift. For those who are unable to come to Shul, you could find a Chumash at home and hold it in your hand and dance! This book is our lifeline. Hug it, kiss it, and ask Hashem to open your eyes to understand it and follow it. It may feel a bit strange, but it will help you connect to Hashem, the Maker of our world.

No matter where you are, Hashem hears, sees and wants a connection with you.

It is For You

PARSHAT LECH LECHA, OCTOBER 2020

Some people feel that they should do the mitzvot because they are doing Hashem a favour by listening to Hashem's instructions. Really, they would rather not get up and have to daven, or give up their hard-earned money to charity. But what can they do? This is what Hashem has asked them to do, so they must.

The truth is that we have an upside-down view of the purpose of the mitzvot, and this prevents us from understanding the power and greatness of each one.

There was once a poor farmer who was walking through a forest. He heard a girl cry out from a deep ditch and ran to help her. It transpired that the girl was a princess and when he brought her back to the palace, the king was extremely grateful. As a reward, he gave the farmer two large sacks and told him to go down into the storehouse and gather many precious stones and gold into the sacks.

The farmer had never seen gold or precious stones and did not realise their value. He was actually quite annoyed with the king for 'rewarding' him by asking him to do hard work, gathering up stones. He had two hours in the storehouse, and spent his time complaining and trying to relax on top of the gold coins. Why should he have to work so hard? He worked hard enough anyway – he might as well have a break in the king's palace.

After two hours, the servants called him to come out and he quickly put into his sack a few gold coins, so that the king would not be disappointed or angry with him.

Only when he returned home, and related the day's events to his family, did they explain what an opportunity he had missed and how he had wasted that precious time in the storehouse.

We have free choice in this world, but Hashem does not need our mitzvot – we do. They are here for us – for our own benefit.

In this world, we are like that farmer. Hashem wants to give to us, but knows that free gifts are uncomfortable to receive. Hashem therefore devised a world where we have an opportunity to earn everlasting reward for the efforts we make in this world. The Torah is full of mitzvot which are like diamonds (only worth much more). We have free choice in this world, but Hashem does not need our mitzvot – we do. They are here for us – for our own benefit.

In Genesis 12, Abraham was asked to leave his birthplace. The words Hashem used were "Lech lecha", Go for yourself. Abraham was asked to leave his birthplace. It was difficult for him, and he did not know why he had to leave, but Hashem knew that Abraham had great potential that could only be reached once he had moved away from his homeland. Hashem was teaching Abraham (and us too) the most important lesson. Even though it may not be easy and we may not understand Hashem's instructions, by following the path of the Torah and keeping Hashem's mitzvot, we ourselves are the ones who benefit the most.

The mitzvot help us to become great people who are deeply connected to Hashem and compassionate towards all people.

May we all merit to utilise our limited time in Hashem's 'storehouse' (aka the world), so that we will feel happy and content when it is time for us to leave it.

What Did I Say?

OCTOBER 2020

Have you ever been asked that question before?

'What did I say?'

You may have been hurt by someone's words and they have no idea why. Perhaps their words brought up a painful memory or maybe their complaints about their life compounded your sense of loss for what you do not have.

They are only words, one might think, but words are more powerful than we realise.

In Genesis 1:3, Hashem said, "Let there be light." And just like that, there was light! How wonderful it would be if our words could create as Hashem's words did. Hashem created the world, and formed human beings with the potential to create too.

Hashem gave us wheat, and we produced bread. Hashem hid coal deep in the ground, and we produced electricity. Hashem created (almost) invisible atoms, and we produced the atom bomb.

This world is full of potential and it is our job to "work it and guard it" (Genesis 2.15). What we do not realise is that when we talk, we create worlds for others to live in.

'You never clean up after yourself. You'll never manage on your own!'

'You'd probably lose your head if it wasn't connected with your neck!'

'Mistakes happen, I'm sure you will get it right next time – what is important is that you tried.'

The words that we say enter the other person's heart and replay continuously in their minds as they struggle to succeed in this world.

The words that we say enter the other person's heart and replay continuously in their minds as they struggle to succeed in this world.

Hashem created the world and placed humans in it with a mandate to continue to build and develop it and ourselves. Every day, we have the capacity to build or destroy, with our mouths alone. Our rabbis say, "Life and death are at the hands of the tongue" (Proverbs 18:21). If only we appreciated how true those words were.

Let us choose to build life together.

Have I Changed at All?

OCTOBER 2020

It's the end of October and the festivals are over. Schedules are back to normal, and winter is slowly creeping up on us.

I can vaguely recall Yom Kippur and the inspiration I gained from the prayers and the new year resolutions. It all seems so far away and I'm ashamed to admit that most days I forget to do what I committed to do each day. It wasn't a large change or major decision. Yet life is so busy and I am swept along with its tide.

The American Society of Training and Development performed a study on accountability and found that you have a 65% of completing a goal if you commit to someone. And if you have a specific accountability appointment with a person you've committed, you will increase your chance of success by up to 95%.

When our goals are in our minds only, they are often pushed aside by events or disruptions that come up in our day. But if we know that we need to report it to someone else, that will give us an incentive to keep on track.

> *When our goals are in our minds only, they are often pushed aside by events or disruptions that come up in our day.*

Perhaps you also made new goals for this year. Are you managing better than me? Or are we on the same page?

Working with a partner encourages us to keep our commitments, and even though I'm disappointed that I haven't managed until now, I am hopeful that through writing this message, we can all learn this important idea, and find friends to help us achieve our goals. Next year, please G-d, may we all be able to answer the question "Have I changed at all?" in the affirmative.

Still Waiting...

PARSHAT VAYESHEV, NOVEMBER 2020

Sometimes, we find ourselves in situations where we are still waiting for our prayers to be answered. Perhaps someone is suffering with mental or physical illness, or waiting to have a child, or find a partner. Every day, seeing people who have what they lack, can lead to feelings of sorrow and isolation.

Sometimes we wait for so long and our hopes are dashed again and again. We cannot see any possible solution and waiting can be so painful.

We need strength to continue praying and hoping. King David wrote "Hope to Hashem, strengthen and fortify your heart and hope to Hashem" (Psalm 27.1).

Why is the phrase "hope to Hashem" repeated?

Many times in life, we pray and we try and it seems that it's not helping. At that point, we need to strengthen ourselves with the faith that Hashem is listening and doing what is best for us, and that Hashem can change the situation in an instant. Only then, can we pray again.

In Parshat Vayeshev, we read about Joseph, who was hated by his brothers. He was thrown into a pit and sold as a slave to a group of travelling merchants. He prayed to Hashem to help him and was then sold as a slave to a rich Egyptian, named Potifar. There, he was given an extremely difficult test, when the wife of Potifar tried repeatedly to seduce him. Joseph withstood the test. One would think that at this point he might be rewarded by Hashem. However, rather than being rewarded, he was thrown into prison for twelve years.

In a moment, his whole life was transformed, and he became the viceroy in Egypt, second only to Pharaoh himself.

Joseph continued to be faithful, despite his terrible circumstances. Twelve years later, he was suddenly released from prison and brought to the king's palace in order to interpret Pharaoh's dreams. In a moment, his whole life was transformed, and he became the viceroy in Egypt, second only to Pharaoh himself.

Joseph never stopped hoping for Hashem's help, and many years later, he was rewarded for his faith and his commitment.

I have a friend who suffered from mental illness for many years. She tried all different kinds of medication and treatment, and her family prayed and helped as much as they could. It was heart-breaking to see her pain and it seemed that there was no solution at all. One day, a different doctor tried a different medication and slowly my friend started to improve and live again. After ten years of hoping, when it seemed like there was no more hope, salvation came and she is now living a functional, happy life.

It is so hard to keep on praying when we don't see results. Hashem can solve our problems in ways we cannot even imagine.

May we merit to see salvation for all those who need it.

BRINGING IT HOME

Hashem hears our prayers in any place, at any time. When lighting Shabbat candles, it is a most propitious time to pray. Ask Hashem for help in whatever is troubling you and continue asking, even when it seems that your prayers are not heard.

Can You Focus?

PARSHAT VAYETZE, NOVEMBER 2020

I am easily distracted.

It's hard for me to focus on what's in front of me, as there are many different tasks on my mind. Admittedly, we are blessed with six children, which means that it is rare for me to be able to have a conversation that is uninterrupted. But still, even without the interruptions, my mind sometimes wanders and I feel bad that I'm not giving my full attention to whatever is on my plate at that moment.

This is actually quite a common phenomenon and, due to technological advances, our average attention span has decreased from 12 seconds in 2000 to 8 seconds in 2019. Our ability to focus on our present task is diminishing, which means that our productivity level is falling too.

When Jacob awoke from his sleep on Mount Moriah, he thought, "Surely the Lord is in this place, and I was not aware of it". He was afraid and said, "How awesome is this place! This is none other than the house of God; this is the gate of heaven" (Genesis 28:12–17). He didn't realise that the place where he slept contained within it a certain holiness, and he almost just passed it by.

There is a beautiful thought in Chassidism which teaches us that every place and person has a spark of holiness inside it. Our job in this world is to uncover that holiness and elevate the person or place.

> *Every place and person has a spark of holiness inside it. Our job in this world is to uncover that holiness and elevate the person or place.*

When we are constantly thinking about yesterday or tomorrow or our next task, we may miss those sparks of holiness that we are witnessing or experiencing right now. To be fully present with one other person may be harder than giving a talk to 100 people. However, each person is like a whole world, and to really listen and give our attention to that person is an unparalleled gift.

There is no large applause, no acclaim or praise. The act of giving of oneself is a private gift that can mean the world of difference to that one person. Their spark of holiness could be ignited with a few kind words of encouragement.

Henny Machlis, of blessed memory, was a great woman who hosted over 200 people every Shabbat. Yet, when I read her biography, what inspired me most about her was how she gave attention to each person she met. Everyone felt like they were her best friend, and she spoke with them as if she had all the time in the world (when she had none!).

Wherever we are, let us learn from Jacob's example and utilise the opportunity of that moment, by focusing on where we find ourselves, right now.

BRINGING IT HOME

Shabbat is an ideal time to practice focusing. Even if one does not keep Shabbat fully, putting one's phone away for the duration of the Shabbat meal, and paying specific attention to one's partner, child or the special food prepared for Shabbat will elevate the experience of the Shabbat meal.

Who Can We Trust?

NOVEMBER 2020

In our attempt to understand the world around us and be up to date with the world's news, we read, watch and listen to the media.

Some of us constantly check the news. Without realising it, we can become completely swept up with what we read, and therefore it's important to be discerning.

Bad news is often more interesting than good news. Some reporters have an agenda and frame quotes from someone's words to support that agenda. Whole media channels are dedicated to promoting their political beliefs, and even the 'neutral' ones find a way to present 'facts' whilst omitting other facts that may put the event into perspective.

So, if we can't always trust the media and our politicians, and we know that doctors and scientists don't have all the answers, what should we do?

King David writes, "Do not trust in princes, in the son of man, who has no salvation. His spirit leaves, he returns to his soil; on that day, his thoughts are lost. Praiseworthy is he in whose help is the God of Jacob; his hope is in the L-rd his G-d" (Psalm 46:3–5).

Continually checking the news does not change reality – it removes us from playing our part in it.

Hashem created the world and has a master plan for it. Continually checking the news does not change reality – it removes us from playing our part in it. It is our job to focus on what is within our control and try to fulfil Hashem's will for us.

A friend of mine lives next door to a self-declared atheist. She avoids discussing any spiritual matters with her, whilst making sure to be a friendly and caring neighbour. A few weeks ago, my friend asked her what her plans were for Christmas. She replied, "It's all up in the air – we can't plan, only G-d knows!"

Challenging times can reduce our trust in those in power. Whoever wins this or that election will not rule the world. Hashem does. Rather than stressing about the news, let us put our faith in Hashem, and concentrate our energy on our own contribution to the world.

What About Our Part?

NOVEMBER 2020

If Hashem runs the world, why should we bother doing anything? If it's all predetermined, then nothing we do can make a difference anyway!

One of my mentors, Sara Yocheved Rigler, taught me the following concept which helped me understand the difference between fatalism and free choice.

We are not in control of what happens to us, yet we are in control of our response. Our free will lies in the thoughts and actions that we choose.

"He made me so angry, I just had to hit him."
"Her words totally broke me, I cannot ever stand in front of a crowd again".

Other people's actions towards us could be extremely upsetting, and yet we still have the free choice to decide what actions to take to heal ourselves and move on.

We do not need to be merely products of our life's experience until now. We have the capacity to choose how we react and behave. In this way, human beings have tremendous potential to effect change in this world. All that is needed is an interest and willingness to try.

The Torah tells us that Hashem promised Avram that he would have children (Genesis 15:3–5): "And Avram said, 'O my Lord G-d, what can you give me if I am childless?' ... And G-d brought him outside and said, 'Look up at the sky and count the stars. Can you count them?' And G-d said to him, 'So shall your children be."

Rav Meir Shapiro asks what somebody would do if they were told to count the stars. One look at the myriad stars in the heavens would tell what an impossible task this was, and they would probably not even bother to attempt it. But that is not what Avram did. When Hashem told him to "look up at the sky and count the stars", that is exactly what he did. He began to count the stars, even though doing so appeared to be impossible. "Koh yihyeh zarecha," Hashem responded. "So shall your children be."

> *No matter how difficult a task may seem, the Jew will not despair. They will try and try and try again.*

Avram's extraordinary trait of eternal optimism, his refusal to acknowledge the impossibility of any task, will characterise his descendants. This will be the hallmark of the Jewish people. No matter how difficult a task may seem, the Jew will not despair. They will try and try and try again.

All that is asked of us is to put in the effort. "Lo alecha hamlacha ligmor, v'lo atah ben chorin l'hivatel mimena" – "You are not expected to complete the task, but neither are you free to avoid it" (Rabbi Tarfon, Ethics of Our Fathers 2:21).

As Eleanor Roosevelt (1884–1962) said, "Remember always that you have not only the right to be an individual; you have an obligation to be one". Each person has their own unique way in which they can contribute to this world, and without it, the world is incomplete.

Having faith in Hashem does not mean that we read the paper, sigh and then rest on our laurels. It means that we work our hardest to repair the world, but without wasting time watching and complaining about those aspects that we cannot change.

Rabbi Sacks, of blessed memory, was a philosophy student who initially had no intention at all of becoming a rabbi. Yet he saw a need and answered the call. He did not know if he would succeed, but he knew that it was his duty and responsibility to try. Years later, his words have inspired thousands of people across the world.

There is so much more each one of us can do, if only we believe in our individual strength and the potential Hashem put inside us.

May we find it and use it wisely.

Living with Laughter

DECEMBER 2020

'll be honest. It's all getting me down. These past few months with Covid-19 have felt like a giant rollercoaster for my emotions. Worry, hope, sadness, relief, frustration, acceptance, and now lots of disappointment. Thank G-d, the vaccine is now being given throughout the country, but another strain (Delta) has arrived, and uncertainty has returned.

I was trying to be organised before the holidays and had written a neat piece about our purpose in the world. However, the events of the last few days, with another possible lockdown imminent, are causing so much pain and worry that I felt that we all need a different kind of message – one that could bring joy and hope.

Bringing cheer to others can literally light up their lives in these dark times.

We Jews are well acquainted with tragedy. We've been through a lot and one of the tools that has helped us is laughter. Yesterday, I shared a funny message with a friend, and we laughed together over the phone. It really lifted my spirits!

'Laughter is the best medicine', or as Proverbs 17:22 says: "A happy heart enhances one's brilliance, and a broken spirit dries the bones".

We might not feel like laughing, and it may even feel callous to laugh whilst life is so difficult for many. Of course, we need to be empathetic towards another's pain, and compassionate when a friend or family member is complaining about their struggles. Yet there is still a place for humour and laughter to help us all get through these stressful times.

The Gemara Taanit (22a) relates a story. Reb Beroka met Eliyahu Hanavi (Elijah the Prophet) in the marketplace and asked him an interesting question: 'Who here has a place in the World to Come?' To which Eliyahu Hanavi responded, 'Nobody'. Shortly afterward, Eliyahu told him, 'These two who are passing by us have a place in the World to Come.' Reb Beroka went over and asked the men what they did for a living. They answered him, 'We are badchanim (jesters). We cheer up depressed people and settle arguments between quarrelling people.'

One would not usually think of jokers as the greatest people in our world, but we underestimate the power of humour to uplift those around us. Bringing cheer to others can literally light up their lives in these dark times.

We all need it, and together we can bring more joy to the world.

Whose Side Are You On?

CHANUKA, DECEMBER 2020

Thanks to the media, peer pressure, music and more, teenagers are expected to always look beautiful.

While that might be acceptable for your favourite fictional high-school comedy on television, those types of standards are often too much for the average teenager.

Many teenagers are at the height of physical awkwardness. They are trying to find out who they are and where they fit into the world, and have trouble trying to be one of the many beautiful teenagers out there.

In Dr Mary Pipher's best-selling book, "Reviving Ophelia", she writes about the social pressures faced by many adolescents in our society today, and the painful illnesses that can result from these pressures. She identifies one of the main culprits as the pressure to be beautiful. She coined the term "lookism", which she defined as "the evaluation of a person solely on the basis of appearance".

In an article entitled 'The Beauty Wars', Rebbetzen Sara Yocheved Rigler talks about this phenomenon and explains that we can trace it back to ancient Greek culture. The Greeks innovated the aesthetic ideal. While other ancient cultures beautified their buildings and pottery, the Greeks introduced the idea of beauty for its own sake, or, as we say today, 'art for art's sake'.

> *The ultimate value of the Greeks was beauty; the ultimate value of the Jews is holiness.*

The Torah identifies the ancestor of the ancient Greeks to be Yefet, one of the sons of Noah. 'Yefet' means beauty. Historian Will Durant, in his book "The Life of Greece", refers to ancient Greece's "infatuation with physical beauty and health", to the exclusion of "the study of character and the portrayal of soul".

Chanuka celebrates the victory of the Jews over the Greeks. The conflict was not only a military war, but even more so a culture struggle between opposing values. The ultimate value of the Greeks was beauty; the ultimate value of the Jews is holiness. Even a cursory glimpse at contemporary Western society reveals that the Chanuka battle isn't over yet.

 FOR THE LAST NIGHT OF CHANUKA THIS YEAR, LET US TAKE A MOMENT TO ASK OURSELVES WHICH CULTURE WE IDENTIFY WITH MORE.

- *Are we constantly concerned with our appearance?*
- *When we meet someone for the first time, do we notice their clothes or their character?*
- *What values do we pass to our children (perhaps subconsciously) when we discuss the news or public figures?*

It is not easy to focus inwards, in a world where the public persona is glorified. Yet, we have our Torah, and we light candles inside our homes, where we can redefine our values.

Holiness is accessible to everyone, and the light inside us shines more brightly than any external beauty.

As Chanuka ends, may we find that light and use it to make the world shine.

The Voice of Hope

PARSHAT SHEMOT, JANUARY 2021

Here we are again...

Back in lockdown. Overflowing hospitals, no school for the children, rising death rates, fear and panic all over.

Globally, there is the shocking storming of the United States Capitol and the threats to its democracy, and Iran is back to enriching their uranium.

The news is dire and it's hard to keep our spirits up at this worrying time.

I'm currently reading a book called "The Power of Bad" by John Tierney and Roy F. Baumeister. It doesn't sound like the best book to be reading at a time like this, but let me quote for you a small segment that fascinated me.

The authors were discussing the negativity bias in our lives. We remember negative experiences more than positive ones. The media constantly updates us with dire predictions and shocking, distressing events that take place around the world, rather than positive news of those surviving, or even thriving.

Have you ever heard of PTSD (post-traumatic stress disorder)?

Many of you will have heard of this condition, but how many of you have heard of post-traumatic growth?

Tierney and Baumeister write in the book the following: "Post-traumatic stress syndrome became common knowledge but not the concept of post-traumatic growth which is actually far more prevalent. Most people who undergo trauma ultimately feel that the experience has made them stronger, wiser, more mature, more tolerant and understanding or in some other way a better person.

"The influential psychologist, Martin Seligman, has often lamented that so much attention is lavished on post-traumatic stress syndrome rather than post-traumatic growth because it causes people to mistakenly expect that bad events will have a mainly negative effect.

"After being exposed to a terrifying event, at least 80% of people do not experience post-traumatic stress syndrome. Even though a bad event is more powerful than a good event, over time, people respond in so many constructive ways that they typically emerge more capable than ever of confronting a life challenge."

Post-traumatic stress syndrome became common knowledge but not the concept of post-traumatic growth which is actually far more prevalent.

Humanity is in crisis at the moment. Each person is suffering in their own way, but it is our attitude towards the situation that will determine our response.

In this week's Parsha of Shemot, the Jewish people are exhausted and depressed from their terrible suffering in Egypt. Amram, the leader of the people, separates from his wife Yocheved, due to the miserable situation. "Why should we bring children into a world like this? If it is a boy, he will be thrown into the Nile."

Amram's six-year-old daughter, Miriam, questioned her father (respectfully, of course).

"The Egyptians are killing our baby boys, but what you are doing is worse. You are also killing the girls!"

Despite the incredibly painful situation, she had a strong belief in Hashem that they would be redeemed and the future would be brighter. She was a lone positive voice in a sea of negativity.

Amram listened to his daughter, and reunited with his wife. They had a child: Moses. This little boy grew up to become the person who Hashem chose to redeem His people and take them out of Egypt.

Each of us can be the "Miriam" of our times. We desperately need "voices of hope", words of encouragement, and words of positivity. Yes, this pandemic seems to be never-ending, but there is a vaccine, and hope is on its way.

We need to search for positive news and spend time focusing on that.

As Tierney and Baumeister state, 80% of people grow from negative experiences. We can focus on our blessings, not our losses. It is not an easy struggle, but we have the ability to choose our words and our focus each day. We can be forces of light and positivity, rather than regurgitating the world's problems over and over amongst ourselves.

Many might have thought that Miriam was engaging in wishful thinking, but it was through her actions that our leader, Moses, was born.

Let us strengthen ourselves, ask Hashem for help, and brighten up the people around us with the voice of hope.

Anger Danger

PARSHAT VAERA, JANUARY 2021

We all get angry sometimes.

It is a human emotion, and throughout the day we experience various disappointments and frustrations, which can lead to anger. The problem with anger is that when we are in this state, we are not actually thinking logically and therefore our decision-making process is hampered.

This is a physiological phenomenon. Dr Harry Mills PhD, an American psychologist, explains that emotions more or less begin inside two almond-shaped structures in our brains called the amygdala. The amygdala is the part of the brain responsible for identifying threats to our wellbeing, and for sending out an alarm when threats are identified, which results in us taking steps to protect ourselves. The amygdala is so efficient at warning us about threats that it gets us reacting before the cortex (the part of the brain responsible for thought and judgment) is able to check on the reasonableness of our reaction.

In Parshat Vaera, we learn about the first seven of the ten plagues. The second of the ten plagues was frogs. Rashi cites a Rabbinic source that describes how this plague manifested itself. At first, one single frog emerged from the river and the Egyptians tried to kill it by striking it. However, instead of harming the frog, it split into swarms of frogs each time it was struck, until the frogs became so numerous that they inundated the land.

Rabbi Gefen quotes the Steipler Gaon (1899–1985) who asks an important question. The Egyptians surely saw that the first time they hit the frog they did not succeed in destroying it. In fact, their hitting had the opposite result, causing more frogs to emerge. Yet they continued to hit the frog many times, filling the whole of Egypt with frogs. Why did they not learn their lesson and refrain from hitting the frog after they saw its disastrous results?

In a moment of anger, we are unable to use our mental faculties efficiently.

The Steipler Gaon explains how the destructive trait of anger causes a person to act. When a person is insulted, they feel the need to avenge this treatment, therefore respond in kind to the aggressor. The aggressor returns the insult, and they in turn feel the need to return the insult again, until both are subject to a vicious circle of fruitless retaliation and a full-blown quarrel erupts, with harmful consequences for all involved.

This is what happened in Egypt. In a moment of anger, they lashed out at the frogs, only to find themselves with more frogs.

In a moment of anger, we are unable to use our mental faculties efficiently. Taking a break (ideally for at least 20 minutes) or moving away from the situation for a while, can give our brains a chance to recalibrate and thereby find solutions to the problem, rather than exacerbate it.

Each week, when we read the Parsha, we learn about other people's actions – both the good and the bad. Science can help us understand what may cause these mistakes, and we can use both the Torah's examples and scientific studies to help us understand and regulate our own emotions, so that we can respond better to the challenges in our lives.

The Bridge of Life

JANUARY 2021

This week in the UK, the death toll from Covid-19 reached a devastating 100,000 people. That's one hundred thousand individual human beings with hopes, dreams, families and friends. Our Rabbis say that one human life is as precious as the whole world. Each person is special and, as a nation, we mourn every loss.

Mourning a loved one is an incredibly painful process, and for many, the isolation due to Covid has made this process even harder.

There is a beautiful Jewish song called "Conversation in the Womb", written by Abie Rotenberg, that may help those who are mourning a loved one*.

In the song, there are twins in the womb, discussing the meaning of their lives. The twins argue about what will happen to them once they leave their mother's womb. Child A believes that there is a future life beyond the womb. Child B, a rational being, can only accept what his own intelligence could grasp. He argues that there is only existence in the world he knows. There is only 'this world', i.e. the womb.

Child A repeats what was transmitted to him, that with the emergence from the womb they will enter a new and more spacious realm. They will eat through their mouths, see distant objects with their eyes,

> **Belief in the next world can comfort us when thinking of our loved one.**

their legs will straighten and they will stand erect. They could even travel vast distances on a gigantic earth filled with oceans and rivers.

Child B only believes in what he can sense and is sceptical of his brother's naivety in indulging in such fantasies. The more the 'believer' elaborates on the wonderful features that they will encounter in the 'next

---

* The song is based on the teachings of Rabbi Yechiel Michel Tucazinsky (1871–1955), who wrote an outstanding work on the theological issues of death and mourning called "Gesher HaChaim" (The Bridge of Life). In this classic presentation, he explains the Jewish position that this world is merely a bridge to the next world. The soul enters the individual before one's life and then lives on to the next world (Olam Haba). Rabbi Tucazinsky's father died in Bulgaria when he was only 8 years old and, in 1882, he immigrated to Jerusalem, where he lived with his grandfather.

world', the more the 'rational' brother ridicules him.

In the middle of one of these arguments, the womb suddenly opens. Child A, the 'naive' one suddenly leaves. Remaining within, Child B is shattered by the tragedy that has overtaken his brother. 'Brother, where are you? How did you leave me?' As he moans his misfortune, he suddenly hears the cry of his brother and he trembles in fear. Is this not the last gasp of his brother as his brother's life comes to an end?

Outside, at that very moment, joy and celebration fill the room as the baby is born into the world: "Mazel tov! Mazel tov! A baby...we have a son!"

It is true that Child A is crying, but those cries are cries of life. Just as the life of the embryo merely constitutes the transition to a broader and more exciting and rich life – so too, we can see life on this earth is merely a prelude to a more glorious life, which we are incapable of conceiving with our limited knowledge. As great as the difference between life inside and outside the womb, the difference which the soul will ultimately experience between this life and the world to come is immeasurably greater. Whilst it is hard for us, in this world, to cope with loss, belief in the next world can comfort us when thinking of our loved one.

I once heard a different analogy that may offer comfort too. Imagine standing at the seashore waving goodbye to a friend travelling on a ship to a beautiful island. Years ago, there was no email or WhatsApp. Moving away meant a loss of communication, and those standing on the shore waving were sad to see them go. Yet the knowledge that they were moving on to a better place eased the pain of separation.

May Hashem comfort all the mourners at this difficult time and may Hashem "wipe the tears off every face" (Isaiah 25:8).

Why Am I Here?

JANUARY 2021

"**W**hat am I doing here? Why do I exist?

A nice, easy, uncomplicated subject. Not.

Could it really be that the purpose of our existence is to study hard, work hard in our jobs, raise children (if we are lucky enough to be given that gift), have nice holidays, give some charity, retire and relax, and then die?

There must be more...

Let's expand the question. "Why did Hashem make the world?"

Rabbi Moshe Chaim Luzatto, the great 16th-century theologian and Kabbalist , explains that Hashem is all good and therefore created the world in order to bestow goodness. Sounds like a lovely idea, but if we look at the world, it may seem like (G-d forbid) the plan failed. The world is indeed a beautiful gift, but we have not done so well in looking after it and perfecting it. There is sorrow and pain, war, illness and tragedy. This is a gift?

Let us look a little deeper. Our rabbis say that "this world is like a corridor to the world to come" (Ethics of Our Fathers 4:16). This world is the place to do, the next world is the place to receive. Have you ever received a free gift? How does it feel? At first, it may seem exciting, but to constantly receive is humiliating.

When a person works hard and receives reward for her efforts, she feels much more satisfied and enjoys the gift so much more than if it was just for free.

Hashem sees and records every step we take towards improvement and rewards us for our efforts.

Hashem wanted to give to us, but knew that we would feel uncomfortable to be given something we didn't deserve. Hashem therefore created this world, where Hashem has hidden behind a veil. Those who do not wish to look deeper will not find Hashem, but those who are searching for the truth will find it.

We are given free choice in this world as to whether to engage with our

spiritual essence and follow the Torah's guidance or not. The rewards in the next world are infinitely greater than we can ever imagine, but we need to use our free choice here to earn them.

But why does this world seem so unfair? Why doesn't Hashem intervene more?

If Hashem would reveal Himself in this world, there would be no more free choice. Imagine a person was struck by lightning whenever they uttered an unkind word? Would that person have free choice? We would be like robots, acting out of fear of punishment. How can one receive reward for doing something without actively choosing to do it?

In order for humankind to complete our purpose in this world, Hashem had to hide to enable us to search for Him and choose to follow His ways. It is true – this world is imperfect, but this is no mistake. We are all imperfect, so that together we can fulfil our potential, improve ourselves and help others too. Hashem sees and records every step we take towards improvement and rewards us for our efforts.

Thus life becomes meaningful and fulfilling. It's not about how much money we earn, what degree we achieved or our social media standing. All of these are extraneous to our primary task. We are here to shine the light of our unique soul into the world and thereby fulfil our personal mission.

May Hashem help us all to discover our unique purpose and fulfil it.

Digging Deep

TU B'SHVAT, JANUARY 2021

It's cold outside. The trees are bare and the sky is grey. In the winter, animals hibernate and in lockdown, we are hibernating too. Staying home and under the covers.

I heard a lovely idea from the teachers at Esti's school that relates to our situation now.

We are currently in the Hebrew month of Shvat, when we celebrate Tu B'Shvat – the birthday of the trees. It seems strange to celebrate trees when all we can see right now are empty branches and bare ground. It all seems to look dead. One would think that the time for celebration is during the spring, when we can see the buds growing and flowers beginning to bloom.

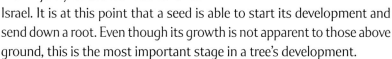

The month of Shvat generally falls in the darkest part of the winter, when the majority of the rain has fallen in Israel. It is at this point that a seed is able to start its development and send down a root. Even though its growth is not apparent to those above ground, this is the most important stage in a tree's development.

Therefore, in essence, Shavat is the perfect month to celebrate the life of a tree. In the heart of the winter, it seems like there is no hope for any tree to survive. In reality, though, this is the time where the tree is actually beginning its life! Hidden under the surface of the ground, the seed is preparing itself to eventually sprout.

On a deeper level, the Talmud explains that a person is compared to a tree. If we ever face times of despair, where we are suffering and everything seems dark and hopeless, then it would help us to understand that this is the time when our most intense growth can come. When the challenges that we face seem so difficult, we need to remember that these dark days of suffering can lead us to grow in ways we never imagined possible, making us into greater people.

In the heart of the winter, it seems like there is no hope for any tree to survive. In reality, though, this is the time where the tree is actually beginning its life!

Looking a little further, we realise that the tree would not be able to flourish if it didn't have that phase where it was in the soil, in the dark. Deep underground it has the ability to spread its roots and strengthen itself, so that it will be able to grow and blossom during the spring.

These days, weeks and months of lockdown have shaken up our entire lives. We are forced to stay at home and redefine our values and our goals. Even though it's hard and uncomfortable, surrounded by mud and hidden from the sunshine, let us try to use this time to strengthen our roots and our homes, so that when spring arrives, we will develop into beautiful people.

BRINGING IT HOME
It is customary to eat 15 fruits on Tu B'Shvat and thank Hashem for the gift of healthy, delicious and diverse fruits provided by trees all over the world. Taking the time to make a blessing on the fruit helps us appreciate the many, often unnoticed, gifts in our lives.

THE BLESSING ON FRUIT IS:
Baruch atah A-donay, Elo-heinu Melech Ha'Olam, borei pri ha'etz.
Blessed are You, L-rd our G-d, King of the universe, who creates the fruit of the tree.

The One Thing We (All) Can Do

FEBRUARY 2021

"Nothing to do. Nowhere to go. The day stretches out before me. No plans can be made. Shops and cinemas are closed. I'm stuck at home with the four walls as my company, and I don't even know when this will end?"

This is not my experience, but it seems to be a common feeling amongst those who are alone or shielding.

We all like to be productive. A busy day feels good, and making plans gives us a sense of purpose. The coronavirus has stripped us of those tools that help us manage our day. We need to look for something else.

Some have advocated learning a new language (Hebrew would be a great one to try!), studying online (Rabbi Sacks, of blessed memory, has some wonderful podcasts) or gardening. All these options are helpful and can fill our day with a certain amount of structure.

Not everyone enjoys the above activities or has the equipment available to facilitate them. It's also hard to motivate oneself when there is no deadline or social pressure to 'be there'.

So what else can we do?

Viktor Frankl, the Holocaust survivor and Austrian psychologist, wrote "When we are no longer able to change a situation, we are challenged to change ourselves."

The one thing that we can all do is give.

Whatever our situation, we all have something to give. Whether it's making a phone call to someone who is home bound, writing a letter to a distant friend, or giving a compliment to a family member who is getting on our nerves, every act of giving is meaningful and uplifting. When we think about ourselves, worry and fear creep in. In contrast, when we think about others, hope and purpose replace those thoughts. We can make a difference. We can brighten up someone else's day. Some people wait all day for the phone to ring; for some human contact.

Human beings need social interaction. More than food and drink replenishes our bodies, the gift of a friend warms the soul. In addition, the beautiful side effect of giving is that in lifting up someone else's spirits, we raise our own spirits too.

In Hebrew, the word to give, 'Natan', is a palindrome. Through giving to others, we give to ourselves.

Even when we are stuck at home, every day we have the op-

> *When we are no longer able to change a situation, we are challenged to change ourselves.*

portunity to be kind to someone else. It needs no fancy equipment, or sophisticated intellectual capacity. Just an open heart and a desire to become a giver. Looking for opportunities to give helps us to view our situation differently, as our focus shifts to what we can do, rather than what we can't. Captain Tom Moore taught us this concept. He was stuck at home just like the rest of us but used this opportunity to find a way to give to others and raised millions of pounds for the NHS.

In the words of Rabbi Dr Abraham Twerski[*], "Love is not about what I am going to get, but what I am going to give. People make a mistake in thinking that you give to those whom you love, the real answer is, you love those to whom you give."

When we give to others, we increase our love for them and spread more joy into the world.

May Hashem help us to utilise this time well, so that one day, when the restrictions are lifted, we will be proud of what we truly achieved during these difficult times.

At the Click of a Button

FEBRUARY 2021

L ast week, Basya asked me what the difference was between a hedgehog and a porcupine.

I did not know the answer, but we were lucky enough to be in a room with a Google Nest, so I asked Google and received a detailed verbal explanation of the difference between the two animals.

We live in a generation where we can find answers to many questions in an instant. No more trips to the library, or inaccessible information

---

* *Rabbi Dr Twerski passed away this week at the age of 90, having just published his 90th book. While serving as assistant rabbi in his father's congregation in Milwaukee in the 1950s, Rabbi Dr Twerski attended medical school at Marquette University. After finishing his residency, Rabbi Dr Twerski spent the next 20 years serving as the clinical director of the department of psychiatry at St Francis Hospital, while also serving on the faculty at the University of Pittsburgh. He was a world-renowned drug and alcohol addiction expert, and in 1972 he founded the Gateway Rehabilitation Center in Pittsburgh. Rabbi Dr Twerski was also one of the first communal leaders to confront the issue of spousal abuse in the Jewish community in his ground-breaking 1996 book, "The Shame Borne in Silence." For more information about Rabbi Twerski, see www.aish.com/ jw/s/Rabbi-Abraham-Twerskis-Copious-Blessings.html*

due to language constraints. Google or Alexa have the answers and, at the click of a button or a simple voice message, we have access to huge amounts of data for free.

Behavioural psychologists bemoan the effect that this has on our society and our mental abilities. They are correct, of course, and there is a danger of us becoming so reliant on these amenities that we are unable to figure out basic problems ourselves. (There is also a danger of harmful and inappropriate information flooding our screens – but that is a topic for another article.)

For today, though, I'd like to focus on the tremendous gift that this phenomenon gives us. When we sit at the computer, we can tap into fantastic learning opportunities and access material that was previously only available to a select few.

I'm amazed at how many kind people take the time to share solutions to common problems, such as how to fix a broken washing machine, or how to repair a tear in one's skirt. Sharing one's experience and knowledge is a kindness that costs nothing but can assist hundreds of people.

Sharing one's experience and knowledge is a kindness that costs nothing but can assist hundreds of people.

This week was half term and we made playdough at home. When trying to choose what to make, we found YouTube videos teaching us step by step how to make a doctor's set and builder's tools. There is so much information available on the internet that can help us in our day-to-day life. I am so grateful to all who have freely shared their knowledge with me and grateful to Hashem for giving people the wisdom to create a platform that makes it possible for them to share.

In Parshat Yitro, we received the Torah: the greatest gift to our people. Filled with instructions as to how to lead our lives, the written Torah is a shorthand transcript of the words that Hashem gave to Moshe. In order to understand the transcript, we need the Oral Law which has been passed down through the generations.

Nowadays, the Torah is translated into many languages. Complicated texts that explain the deeper meaning of our Torah are freely displayed on websites, with explanations from contemporary leaders who define terms in a way that we can easily understand.

Inspirational and educational podcasts, YouTube videos, audio recordings (three-minute sound bites or longer, more detailed classes) are free to download and listen to, at any time of day or night. We can listen or watch whilst exercising, during a car journey or even whilst ironing. Rather than filling our heads with more depressing news about the pandemic, we can use that time to learn Torah and rejuvenate our souls.

When we open up our smart phones and computers, let us make sure to avail ourselves of the wonderful opportunity that we have been given to access the Torah's timeless wisdom, which has the power to enlighten and inspire us. This way, we can infuse ourselves and families with positivity and hope.

As the American author, Brian Herbert, wisely said "The capacity to learn is a gift; the ability to learn is a skill; the willingness to learn is a choice."

May we choose wisely.

Building a Palace

PARSHAT YITRO, FEBRUARY 2021

Three men were working in a quarry cutting stones. The first one was asked what he was doing and he answered simply: "I am cutting stones". The second was asked the same question and answered: "It's my livelihood". In other words, he had a higher purpose than the first man. He was not just cutting stones but receiving compensation in order to buy food and clothing. The third one was asked what he was doing and he answered: "I am building a palace!". He had the vision to see how his seemingly ordinary activity would create something big and important.

The three of them were doing the same thing, but each one grasped the meaning of it in a different way.

Sivan Rachav Meir quotes Rabbi Sacks, who told this story in relation to the mitzvot given to us at Mount Sinai. It's possible to look upon the mitzvot solely as a collection of technical acts, but a deeper look reveals that these acts are the means of perpetuating the eternal message of Mount Sinai.

The mitzvot of the Torah are split into those between fellow people (such as being honest in business, not stealing and judging favourably) and those between people and G-d (such as prayer, keeping Kosher, Shabbat and festivals). It is easier for us to relate to those laws between people. They are mostly intuitive and we can understand that society cannot function without them.

The laws between us and Hashem, however, are harder to follow. We cannot see the results of these acts, and we may not even feel like we are building anything. The spiritual world is hidden, and thus we cannot see how these acts affect the world at all.

I recently heard a story that took place a few months ago, which I'd like to share with you.

Ben received a call from Jack (not their real names), inviting him to come over for a Seudat Hodayah, a 'thanksgiving' party. Ben was grateful for the invitation, but curious as to why he was invited, since he didn't know Jack well at all.

A couple of days later, Ben attended Jack's party and saw 18 people whom he didn't know. It seemed an odd crowd of random people, and he began chatting to the person next to him. His neighbour explained that he was also unsure as to why he was invited, as he barely knew Jack either.

Whilst they were talking, Jack stood up to speak.

"A few weeks ago, I was terribly ill with Covid, and was taken into hospital for treatment. I hovered between life and death and at one point, I felt myself moving upwards. I met my mother, who is no longer alive.

She said to me, "What are you doing here? You don't belong here, go back down!"

I responded, "I'm not well, I can't go back down".

At this point, she told me to

look around. I saw all of you, individually, in your own homes, at that very moment, saying Tehillim (Psalms) for me. Your prayers were bringing me back down into this world.

You may not have realised it, as you had probably been sent a WhatsApp or email text asking you to pray for someone, and you may not have even known who I was. But you prayed for me and I saw you, and your prayers, and I am here today because of you."

It's possible to look upon the mitzvot solely as a collection of technical acts, but a deeper look reveals that these acts are the means of perpetuating the eternal message of Mount Sinai.

Unfortunately, we are all aware of stories where prayers were not answered* and so many have died due to this terrible pandemic. We do not know why some survive, whilst others do not. But this story spoke to me and gave me hope, because of the surprise of those involved. The spiritual world is mostly hidden, but occasionally Hashem lifts up the mask in order to help us understand how every action we do really does affect the world, even though we cannot see it at the time.

We may not realise it, but by following Hashem's laws (even the ones we don't understand), we are creating positive change in this world.

May Hashem help us all to remember this and continue to "build a palace" from our good deeds.

BRINGING IT HOME

1. When you hear of someone who is ill, or someone who needs help (and you cannot physically help them), say a prayer for them. If you can, try to learn one chapter of Tehillim (Psalms) so that you could say it easily, when you feel that you need to pray. Some of you may be familiar with one or two. Prayers can be said in English too.

2. Try to perform a small mitzva this week, between you and Hashem. Whilst doing so, remind yourself of how valuable it is, even though you cannot see its effect.

---

* *For a more detailed discussion on this topic, see 'Why Didn't You Answer My Prayers?' on page 41.*

Me, Myself and I

MARCH 2021

"Love yourself first, because that is who you will be spending the rest of your life with."

Author unknown

When you are waiting in line, going for a walk or taking a bus, what do you do to fill the time? Do you immediately turn on the radio, scroll through your messages or listen to a podcast?

We live in a world full of distractions. We busy ourselves constantly with important tasks (and honestly, some not so important tasks) and fill our time with activities throughout the day. Waiting around for others is frustrating, but as long as we have our smartphones to keep us busy, we are distracted from the feeling of impatience.

Stripped away from those distracting devices, you may have to come face to face with the one person you don't want to meet. Yourself.

A shocking study revealed that 67% of men and 25% of women would prefer to give themselves an electric shock rather than sit in a room alone, bored.[*]

Rabbi Dr Twerski was the Head Psychiatrist in an incredibly busy hospital, responsible for over 300 patients. His work schedule was intense. His supervisor recognised the signs of burnout and sent him to recuperate in a relaxing spa. After six minutes in the whirlpool, Rabbi Twerski began to become restless and tried to leave. The attendant informed him that he must complete 25 minutes in the whirlpool in order to move on to the next part of his treatment. Not wanting to forfeit his payment, he went back in and found himself counting down the minutes until he could escape.

Writing about this experience afterwards,[**] Rabbi Twerski explained

* www.sciencemag.org/news/2014/07/people-would-rather-be-electrically-shocked-left-alone-their-thoughts
** www.aish.com/sp/pg/48891172.html

that although he was busy all day caring for others, there were parts of himself that he did not like. Sitting in the whirlpool with no distractions was extremely painful for him, as he had to face who he really was – and he was unhappy with what he found.

Stripped away from those distracting devices, you may have to come face to face with the one person you don't want to meet. Yourself.

Hashem created each one of us, and we are here in this world for a purpose. We all have positive and negative character traits. Our purpose is to recognise and accept both parts of our personality, and work with them to improve. Only when we are quiet, can we truly look inside ourselves and see who we are now and what we could be. This experience may be painful, but as long as we do this compassionately, recognising that we are all born imperfect and Hashem loves us anyway, then we can commence this most important process of spiritual growth.

The Torah commands us: "You shall love your neighbour as yourself" (Leviticus 19:18). In order to fully love your neighbour, you must be able to love yourself first, and then show your neighbour the kind of love you would want given to you.

This Shabbat, take a few minutes to sit quietly alone and hopefully you will find yourself in great company.

Shabbat. It Saved Our Life

MARCH 2021

We are creatures of comfort. We like things nice and easy, and want life to run smoothly.

If we look at the Torah, it seems that Hashem is asking so much of us. For example, it's not easy to be careful with our speech, and it takes effort and sacrifice to try to keep Shabbat.

Asher Zvi Hirsch Ginsberg (1856–1927), better known as Ahad Ha'am, was one of the foremost pre-State Zionist thinkers. He famously made the remarkable statement, "More than Jews have kept Shabbat, Shabbat has kept the Jews." He may have found this idea from a popular Shabbat song with the following words: "When I guard the Shabbat, G-d will safeguard me."

I recently heard an amazing story that took place about eight years ago to Yitzchak and Albert Farhi, two Jews from New York. The brothers owned a diamond store in Manhattan and one Friday evening they both received a call from their security company. As it was Shabbat, they did not pick up the phone. A call from the security company means that the store may have been broken into and possibly the safe too. It was very stressful for the brothers, as all their precious jewellery was locked in that safe and it was worth half a million of dollars. They did not even have insurance as it was too expensive. This was their total livelihood.

Yet the brothers did not want to break Shabbat. Throughout that Friday night, the security company called again and again, but Yitzchak and Albert worked hard on themselves to strengthen their faith in Hashem and did not pick up the phone or travel to the store.

Finally, when Shabbat was over, their mother called. She had also received those calls and wanted to know whether her sons had gone to the store. They explained that they valued Shabbat more than their business and they were on their way there now. Both brothers were extremely nervous to see what state their store would be in and what had happened to their many years' worth of work.

Once they arrived, they saw that the front window had been smashed and the store was a wreck. All the jewellery on the shelves were stolen. They had lost thousands of dollars. The main issue, though, was the safe, where most of the merchandise was stored. One brother walked towards the safe with trepidation... what would he find? Thank G-d, the safe had not been touched and when he entered the code for the lock, he found everything was in place. They were both incredibly relieved and started cleaning up the mess.

Moments later, a police officer arrived and questioned them.

"Who are you?"

"We are the owners of the store and we were burgled."

The officer replied, "But you were burgled last night! Why didn't you come then?"

They explained about Shabbat and he looked at them incredulously. "You do not realise how lucky you are!", he said. He took them upstairs, into the loft. There, hidden in the corner, was a pile of guns. The police officer described what had taken place the night before.

"These burglars are professionals. Their plan was to lure you into the store so that you would open the safe for them. After taking all the merchandise from the shop front, they went up into the loft to fiddle with the security wires so that the alarm would be triggered, and you would be called. Their plan was to shoot you once you had opened the safe. All through the night, they tried again and again to trigger the alarm and waited for you to arrive. Eventually, at about 4am, they gave up and left. Because it was your Shabbat and you didn't come, your lives were saved!"

"More than Jews have kept Shabbat, Shabbat has kept the Jews."

We think that we are doing Hashem a favour by keeping Shabbat, but Hashem told us that Shabbat is the source of all our blessings. Hashem created the world and loves us enough to give us instructions as to how to live in it. We don't always see 'open' miracles such as the one above, but if we follow Hashem's laws, let us remember that we are the ones who benefit the most.

As with all the mitzvot, Shabbat is not 'all or nothing'. Any steps we take towards making Shabbat more special is precious in the eyes of Hashem and will bring blessing into our lives.

Objective Reality

PARSHAT BESHALACH, APRIL 2021

Back in the days when we were allowed to come together to learn, I conducted a little experiment with a group of women who came to our learning group in Shul.

We passed around a picture of a large, messy room, filled with all different items. Each person shared with the group what they saw in the picture. Some saw the overall mess, whereas others found particular items within the mess.

Our eyes all saw the same picture, yet our minds chose which parts of the picture to focus on. It was fascinating to observe and taught me an important lesson in objective reality.

Nathan Heflick, a senior lecturer in psychology at Lincoln University, commented: "What people think is true is often not true. We tend to think that how we see and view things reflects an objective reality, but this is often not the case."

We do not see things as they are. We see things as we are. Our vision of the world is dependent on many factors, such as how we are feeling at that moment or what issues we are dealing with at the time. For example, those looking into buying a car will notice the different types of cars on the road. An architect will notice the structures of the buildings she passed, and someone who has just lost a loved one will notice – painfully – how many couples there are walking down the road. All are walking down the same road, but they see different realities.

In Parshat Beshalach, the Jewish people are on their journey from Egypt to Israel through the desert. Hashem performed so many miracles for them and sustained them every day with food (manna) and water. Yet, they were continually grumbling about their problems along the way.

Along the journey, we are told "The Jews came to Marah, but they could not drink the waters because they were bitter" (Exodus 15: 23). In the plain sense, the verse refers to the water and explains why the people could not drink it. The Kotzker Rebbe, however, explains homiletically that the reference is to the people: they were bitter. Because the people were bitter, they found fault with the water.

We do not see things as they are. We see things as we are.

We may think that we are being objective and seeing the world as it is. However, the world is multi-faceted. We see what we choose to see, and it isn't easy to change our vision. The good news is that if we are open and willing to look at life differently, then our friends can help us by offering alternative perspectives.

During my experiment in Shul, the women were given the opportunity to look at the picture again, after hearing what everyone else saw. Many were surprised to now see different items in the same picture.

There are many challenges in life, but life can also be beautiful if we open our eyes and learn to focus on the positive aspects of our experience. This Shabbat, may we merit to search for, and find, the good in our lives.

We Are All Human

PARSHAT SHMINI, APRIL 2021

Have you ever found yourself in a bad mood? Do you get frustrated easily? Or are you generally quite calm, but some things bother you intensely and it's hard to calm down?

Then you are in great company. Even the greatest person who ever lived, Moshe, our leader, became angry. The Torah does not gloss over the mistakes of our leaders. The details are all there for everyone to see. "There is no person so righteous on earth that they do good and never sin (Ecclesiastes 7:20). We are all human.

The question is: what do we do when we fail or when we are criticised? Do we react defensively and pass the blame onto someone else? Or do we admit our failings and work on correcting them?

In this week's Parsha, Moshe is upset with his brother, Aaron, for not fulfilling Hashem's commandments correctly. He rebukes Aaron's sons, rather than embarrass his brother directly, and Aaron responds by explaining his reasoning. The verse then states: "and Moshe heard and he agreed" (Leviticus 10:20).

Despite Moshe's anger, he listened carefully and admitted that he, himself, was wrong. He was the leader of the entire Jewish people, and it took great humility to back down and acknowledge that his own understanding of the law was mistaken.

Many times in our life we will make mistakes, or argue with another person. Life happens, and we will lose our cool. The sages said: "The place where the Baal Teshuva (one who has repented) stands, the wholly righteous could not stand." The person who struggles, makes mistakes, but gets back up again and makes amends is greater than one who never had the struggle in the first place. Don't let your failures hold you down. You can view them differently. As Winston Churchill remarked, "Success is the ability to go from failure to failure without losing your enthusiasm".

> *"The place where the Baal Teshuva (one who has repented) stands, the wholly righteous could not stand."*

Berating ourselves, or having too high expectations of ourselves, only leads us to feel self-hatred and frustration. On the other hand, accepting ourselves for our failures enables us to face them honestly and look for ways to improve.

So next time you find yourself falling into anger, remind yourself that you are human. Ask Hashem to help you out of it, and take whatever steps you can to bring yourself back to where you want to be.

A Time and a Place

PARSHAT EMOR, APRIL 2021

"There is a time and a place for everything."

This is an often-quoted idiom that implies that we should hold our emotions in check and only release them at the right moment. However, we are not robots, and our emotions can sometimes overwhelm us.

I recently read a beautiful article by Ruchi Koval, an author and educator from Cleveland, who outlines her method for allowing herself to feel her emotions without permitting them to overtake her.* She describes herself putting those emotions into a locked box during the day and opening the box at night. This way she gives space to herself to grieve or feel anger or any negative emotion, whilst still maintaining a positive aura when interacting with others.

In this week's Parsha, we are taught about all the different festivals. There is Succot, where we are encouraged to rejoice; Yom Kippur, for quiet reflection; Shavuot (when the Jewish people collected the wheat harvest), for thanksgiving. Every holiday has its own emotion and the Hebrew word for festival is 'Moed', meaning 'a fixed time', reminding us of the idiom above. Timing is key.

> *Choosing the appropriate time to acknowledge and express our feelings will ensure that our relationships remain healthy and nurturing.*

One may feel that it is impossible to hold back from displaying strong emotions. This false idea can be easily refuted when observing a teenager – mid-tantrum – opening the door to a friend. She may not have been able to calm down whilst talking to her brother, but the moment she is exposed to potential embarrassment, she immediately manages to hold back her angry words.

* *www.aish.com/sp/pg/Learning-to-Cry.html?s=hp*

King Solomon, in Ecclesiastes 3, offers various examples of emotions that need to be expressed at certain times in our lives: "... A time to weep and a time to laugh; a time of wailing and a time of dancing... A time to love and a time to hate; a time for war and a time for peace".

We cannot be happy all the time and we need to recognise and deal with negative emotions as they rise up within us. Yet, we must be mindful of our environment and how our words and actions can affect others. Choosing the appropriate time to acknowledge and express our feelings will ensure that our relationships remain healthy and nurturing.

Whatever emotions you may be feeling right now, may Hashem help you to manage them, so that you can rule over them, rather than let them rule over you.

What's Mine is Mine

MAY 2021

A story is told about a wealthy Jew who was asked by his grandson how much money he owned.

He replied, saying an amount that was way below his net worth. His grandson was surprised and questioned his calculations.

The wealthy Jew explained as follows. "The amount I told you is the money that I have given to charity. Only that money truly belongs to me, for no one can take that mitzva away from me. All the rest of the money that is now in my possession can be lost, or misused, or become worthless. Money comes and money goes. The money I give away to help others is really the only money I own."

The Hebrew word for an ancient Jewish silver coin in 'zuz', which means 'move'. We all know of people who were millionaires and suddenly lost all their money, and seemingly random individuals who became extremely wealthy overnight.

It is our responsibility to be financially prudent and look after whatever money and possessions Hashem has blessed us with. Yet at the same time, just like our talents, our money is also 'on loan' from Hashem. If we have the opportunity to give some away, let us remember that it is the best investment we will ever make – and Hashem promises us a great return. It is not easy for a person to part with their hard-earned money, but if we remember where it truly comes from, we will find it easier to give.

Money comes and money goes.

In this week's Parsha, we read "Everyone's holy things shall belong to him; whatever a person gives to the Cohen shall be theirs" (Numbers 5:10). The wording is difficult to understand: Whatever they give to the Cohen will be theirs?? Reading between the lines, we can see that the Torah is actually teaching us the fundamental concept that whatever we give away, truly belongs to us.

Over the past year, there have been a large number of online charity appeals, and I have been so inspired as I watched the numbers of donations steadily rise and reach the charity's target. "Mi K'Amcha Yisrael?" "Who is like your people, Israel?" Even after so many campaigns, we still open our hearts and give.

May Hashem bless us with ample sustenance, so that we can continue to give freely to help those in need.

Attitude of Gratitude

PARSHAT BEHA'ALOTECHA, MAY 2021

A while ago, a man in Israel had to travel to America to receive an artificial heart transplant. He was told that the cost of the transplant would be approximately a million dollars. When Rabbi Druk from Jerusalem heard about this, he wondered aloud, "If an artificial heart is worth a million dollars, how much is a real heart worth?"

He continued, "Imagine someone would go over to that patient and tell him he wanted to cover the full cost of that heart transplant and give him a million dollars. How much gratitude would that patient have towards that most generous individual?

"If a person has a working, healthy heart, surely they should be thanking Hashem far more for that gift than the patient would thank that person. Our heart only works because Hashem is making it work. Hashem is deciding on a second-to-second basis that it should function properly and do its job."

In Parshat Beha'alotecha, the Jews are in the desert. They are surrounded by clouds to protect them and provided with an amazing food supply system called 'manna', dropped from heaven each day. The manna tasted of anything they desired and was enough for each family.

Yet the people started grumbling. "We are sick of this food – we want meat!" (Numbers 11:4). After a year's worth of manna, they had grown accustomed to getting this special food, and started complaining about it, rather than appreciating it. We might think that if we had manna from heaven, we would not complain, but the truth is that we do complain about the gifts in our lives – and often.

It takes a conscious effort to stop oneself mid-thought and contemplate the many blessings that we enjoy in this world. Those who do make that effort will find themselves feeling more joy in their lives.

"If an artificial heart is worth a million dollars, how much is a real heart worth?"

In the thanksgiving prayer of Hallel, we say "Hodu L'Hashem Ki Tov, Ki L'Olam Chasdo", "Praise to Hashem for Hashem is good, for Hashem's kindness is forever".

I recently heard a lovely explanation of this phrase: If we (look for and) praise Hashem for good, then we will always merit to see (and appreciate) Hashem's kindness forever. It is not that difficult events don't happen to those who are grateful; rather it is that the person themselves will see life differently and will notice the good more than the troubles.

Recent scientific studies corroborate these Torah ideas. People who regularly write down the things for which they are grateful (which I call 'gratitudes') were found to exhibit higher levels of happiness in life. It was not the circumstances that changed; it was their attitudes towards those circumstances.

For the last couple of years, I have worked with a 'Gratitude buddy'. Each night, we send each other our gratitudes for that day. I truly feel that this exercise has changed my mindset in so many ways. (We do also kvetch to each other sometimes – that's also helpful!). I have learnt from my buddy's gratitudes to see gifts I didn't even notice, and the discipline of writing my gratitudes each day has forced me to find the good in things even on days where I wasn't always in the mood to do so.

May Hashem help us all to see the good and appreciate the many blessings in our lives.

What Are You Looking At?

SEPTEMBER 2021

Yesterday we went on our Sukkot outing with the family. Thank G-d, it was a beautiful day with lovely sunshine, and hopefully everyone enjoyed our day out.

Whilst I was waiting for one of the children, I noticed a young couple sitting near each other with a toddler in a buggy nearby. Both parents were looking at their phones, and the child was talking to them, but they were only giving half answers. The child was so beautiful and so cute, and I felt bad for her.

I know it's easy for me to write about this when watching someone else, but in all honesty, I'm sure there are many times where I am busy doing the same thing!

Phones are extremely helpful at building relationships with those far away, but can sometimes be harmful to those who are right there, by our side.

Sukkot is a time where we take ourselves out of our permanent homes and move in to a temporary shelter with a roof made out of leaves. Here we can feel our vulnerability and the temporality of our existence.

The precious moments of our lives are fleeting and if we don't catch them, recognise, and savour them, they will pass us by, never to return.

Hashem has given us this life, and Covid has taught us that we do not know from moment to moment how it could change.

> *The precious moments of our lives are fleeting and if we don't catch them, recognise, and savour them, they will pass us by, never to return.*

When we sit in our cosy homes, we can become complacent and secure. It is here in the Sukkah, where we allow ourselves to feel the fresh air on our faces and the cold ground beneath us, that we realise we are guests in Hashem's world, rather than hosts inviting Hashem to come and visit our homes. As a guest, we feel humble and grateful for every happy moment, whereas as a host, we feel we own it and deserve it.

Even if one does not have a Sukkah, one can still take a few moments to visit someone else's Sukkah, and feel Hashem's warm embrace as we enter into Hashem's home.

When we take the four species and hold them together, we also remind ourselves that Hashem created nature for us to look after, use and enjoy.

Rina Shnerb, a young teacher, was murdered a few years ago in a terrorist attack in Israel. She was intensively involved with our enslavement to cell phones. As a high-school student, she felt that they had taken control of us, instead of our being in control of them. She was constantly thinking of ways to decrease our screen time while promoting simple human interactions with others.

Her family has continued her efforts and, before Sukkot, they publicized the following message: "Disconnect in order to connect". Specifically, they encouraged us to enter the Sukkah without our cell phones in order to enjoy quality Sukkah time without them.

This Sukkot, let us try to listen to Rina's message and find the time to be fully 'there' with our loved ones, so we can enjoy the gift of their presence in our lives.

Please Forgive Me?

SEPTEMBER 2021

As Yom Kippur is approaching soon, I wanted to ask you forgiveness for anything I may have said, or maybe something I didn't say!

Working with the community is an awesome privilege, but also a huge responsibility, and I hope and pray that I haven't offended or upset you in any way. If I have, then please forgive me.

We are coming up to one of the most precious days of the year.

Yom Kippur is an incredible gift that allows us to spend a whole day editing our life's script. Our rabbis explain that at the end of our life, we will have an opportunity to watch the show consisting of every detail of our lives in technicolour. Not only that, but our thoughts will also be displayed for all to see, a bit like those speech bubbles in cartoon books.

This experience can either be delightful or excruciating, depending on what actions or thoughts we had during our lifetime. The gift of Yom Kippur is that, for one whole day, we stop this script from running, and we sit quietly (in shul or at home) and edit the text. Hashem has given us this time to look through the film and see which parts we'd like to remove.

Here we sit, in the editor's seat, with all the technology available to rewind, delete and replace. The process of 'Teshuva', returning to Hashem, is not an easy one, but once fulfilled properly it has the power to alter those mistakes that we wished we never made.

 THE PROCESS INVOLVES FOUR STEPS (ACCORDING TO MAIMONIDES):

1. *Stopping the sin. We cannot remove a part from the show if we are still currently involved in the same behaviour.*

2. *Admitting the sin before Hashem. Saying aloud what we did wrong and apologising for it.*

3. *Sincere regret. Hashem knows what is in our heart, and sincerity can only be measured by the person themselves.*

4. *Plan for the future. When we do something wrong, it affects our soul and makes it harder for us not to fall into that hole again. In order to really change, we need to make a concrete plan of how to achieve that change.*

In order to help us focus on this amazing day of Yom Kippur, Hashem told us to quieten down our physical 'voice' by abstaining from physical activity. We do not eat or drink, nor do we wash or put perfume on ourselves, or wear leather shoes. We also refrain from all cooking and work, just like on Shabbat.

The gentle voice of our soul is so often drowned out by the loud demands of our physical body (and by the constant noise of our devices). On Yom Kippur, we switch it all off, so that we can tune into our inner voice, which sees far beyond the physical

Here we sit, in the editor's seat, with all the technology available to rewind, delete and replace.

needs of the moment. Our soul senses what feels right, and when we stop and listen to it, we can see which parts of our own film need editing.

This Yom Kippur, may we merit to hear this voice, enjoy the editing process, and emerge with a life's film that we feel proud to watch.

A Fractured People

PURIM, FEBRUARY 2021

A friend of mine was recently in a shop when she saw someone not wearing a face mask. Many people are understandably upset when they see this. My friend is the type of person who stands up for what is right and she therefore went up to the person, rather indignantly, and asked them to please put on a mask. The person replied that they could not, as they suffer from asthma and wearing a face mask affects their breathing.

Covid has affected us in so many ways, and I like to think that we have become kinder and more caring to others. However, there are many people with strong opinions about the best way to handle the pandemic and, as such, they can sometimes relay their message in a rather forceful tone.

Today, we celebrate Purim. It is a beautiful, joyous holiday where we thank Hashem for saving us from Haman's decree to wipe out the Jewish people. When the Book of Esther describes the conversation between Haman (the Prime Minister of Persia) and Achashverosh (the King of Persia), it uses the following words: "There is one nation scattered and dispersed among the nations" (Esther 3:8). Our rabbis explain that we were not unified. There were arguments amongst our people, and this was what gave Haman the power to create such a terrible plan for us.

Later in the story, when Esther was about to plead for our people, she told them to: "Go and gather all the Jews who are in Shushan" (Esther 4:16) and pray for success. Together, we are powerful. Apart, we are weak. How can we find ways to reunite, when we feel so strongly that others are doing wrong?

We cannot judge another until we are in their shoes – and honestly, we never will be.

In his book, "Brain Drain: The breakthrough that will change your life", American doctor, Charles F Glassman wrote, "Judging others is easy because it distracts us from the responsibility of judging ourselves". The first step is to remember that we are not always aware of the full picture. We cannot judge another until we are in their shoes – and honestly, we never will be. Each person's life experience, upbringing and personal character traits are unique.

Let us not be so quick to judge others and let us work together on finding the good in those around us. It is so easy to criticise, but true greatness arises from making the effort to seek to understand another.

Who Am I?

PESACH, MARCH 2021

A few weeks ago, a good friend of mine, Dr Agnes Kaposi, had a debate with another Holocaust survivor, Joan Salter, about whether they should encourage their children to continue to tell their stories to the next generation.

What do you think?

On the one hand, we want these memories to be preserved, but on the other hand, why burden the next generation with the problems of the past?

The two survivors had totally different experiences during the Second World War:

Joan Salter MBE was born Fanny Zimetbaum in Brussels in 1940. She was separated from her parents at the age of 4 and sent to live in America with some very kind foster parents. At the age of 7, she was returned to her 'real' parents, who had survived the war and now lived in the UK. She did not recognise them, and they spoke different languages. For many years, she struggled with her true identity, as she travelled between both sets of parents.

Dr Agnes Kaposi was born in Hungary in 1932, a year before Hitler came to power. She started school at the outbreak of the war. Many of her friends were murdered in the Holocaust, together with half a million other Hungarian Jews, but a series of miracles and coincidences allowed her to survive. Near the end of the war, her family were among almost half a million Hungarian Jews destined for Auschwitz. She found out decades later how it happened that, uniquely, their train was diverted to a labour camp instead.

The retelling of the story of our past is not for us to merely look back and remember. Its purpose is to reignite our faith in Hashem, and help us understand our place in this world.

When discussing her experiences, Agnes told me that she felt that she was the 'luckier' one, as Joan lost her identity, whereas she had a strong family bond that anchored her throughout her many challenges.

We do not always realise the gift that a sense of identity gives us.

When we tell the Pesach story, we are helping ourselves and our children understand that sense of identity: where we came from, what happened to our parents and grandparents, and why we are here today. The retelling of the story of our past is not for us to merely look back and remember. Its purpose is to reignite our faith in Hashem, and help us understand our place in this world.

Throughout the generations, many nations have tried to destroy us. Yet we are still standing here today. This is not a coincidence in history – this is a Divine promise. The Jewish people are eternal and will survive against all odds.

Yet we must remember that we are given this promise in order for us to continue our mission of becoming a people who are worthy of G-d's name. We are 'The People of The Book'. We are to learn from it and pass on its message to future generations. In short, by retelling our people's story on Seder night, we instil that identity into our hearts. With this firm foundation in place, we can then strive to keep Torah values and live spiritually, honestly and correctly, as an example to others. If we are blessed with children, this is the message that we aim to 'pass over' on Seder night to those precious souls.

Wishing you a beautiful and meaningful Pesach!

It's So Easy

APRIL 2021

I hope you are enjoying the Matza and the recent beautiful weather. I feel like we were all just given a little hug from Hashem, as Hashem gave us that small window of the last few days of stunning weather, at exactly the same time as we were allowed to meet another family outside. The last three days are called Chol Hamoed (the intermediary days of Pesach) where we tend to go out on outings, and this year, it also coincides with Easter holidays, so many people were able to enjoy some relaxed time outside in the fresh air.

Thank You, Hashem!

There are many different tasks that we all need to accomplish through-out the year. Some jobs are simple (like tying your shoelace), and some take many hours of hard work (like earning a living). "Rabbi (Yehudah HaNassi) used to say; 'Be careful about how you do a small mitzva, just

as if it were a big one, for you do not know the reward of mitzvot'. (Ethics of Our Fathers 2:1). When it comes to mitzvot, we are not aware of their true value and might just ignore the 'simple' ones.

As American basketball coach, John Wooden, explains, "It's the little details that are vital. The little things are what make big things happen."

One way of translating the word mitzvot is 'connectors'. They connect us to Hashem – the Creator of the world. We cannot always feel that connection, but the more mitzvot we fulfil, the stronger the bond.

Pesach is an example of a difficult mitzva. It takes time, effort and money. All over the world, many Jews keep this mitzva because they value its role in maintaining Jewish identity. It is worth all that effort, because we can see the impact on ourselves and our families.

In contrast, today, I'd like to remind you about an incredibly easy mitzva. It takes about 10 seconds and only involves our mouths. This mitzva is called 'Sefirat HaOmer' – the counting of the Omer. There are seven weeks between Pesach and Shavuot. Our mitzva is to count those days. For example, today's mitzva is to say aloud "Today is Day 5 of the Omer". Simple as that! When we move past day 7, then the text becomes (for example) "Today is Day 8, which is one week and one day of the Omer".

> *"Be careful about how you do a small mitzva, just as if it were a big one, for you do not know the reward of mitzvot."*

Leaving Egypt on Pesach was Hashem's gift to us. Hashem saved us from slavery and gave us our freedom. Seven weeks later, on Shavuot, Hashem asked us if we want to accept the Torah and become Hashem's people. We said 'Yes!' and the rest, as they say, is history.

It was a momentous occasion, and we celebrate it together each year. Counting the days from Pesach to Shavuot reminds us that we are grateful that we made that choice, and thereby became a Jewish nation – Hashem's people.

The text can be said in Hebrew or English and there is a blessing to say before, but some rabbis say that it is better not to say the blessing unless we count every day. So, if you might forget one day (I often do), or if you didn't start from the beginning, then it is better to count the Omer without the blessing.

On page 49 I discussed the immense power of one single mitzva. No matter what your level of religiosity, or how busy your day is, this is one mitzva that we can all fulfil with ease.

Happy counting!

Humility is Key

SHAVUOT, MAY 2021

"I'm no good at anything - don't ask me to help, I wouldn't know how!"

"Look at my award for excellence in music - I've known how to sing since I was 5!"

At first glance, it seems that the first person is humble and the second person is arrogant. However, true humility does not mean negating one's talents or successes. It is more connected to a person's attitude towards their own achievements and towards others successes too.

On Shavuot, we received the Torah - Hashem's greatest gift to the world. It was a monumental moment for mankind and one would have expected the experience to take place in majestic surroundings. However, the Torah tells us that it took place in the wilderness. Empty. Barren. Plain.

Our rabbis explain that this was to teach us that greatness grows from humility. Not from noise and fanfare. Not from singing our own praises. From an open, empty space, where we take the raw materials with which we were born and use them in the correct way to elevate ourselves and help others.

We need to recognise our talents, but realise that they come from Hashem. They are "on loan" to us and should be utilised wisely. If I have a good brain - that is Hashem's gift for me to use to educate others. If I have musical talent - it is also a gift that I can use to uplift those who are suffering. We are all talented at something and our job is to develop ourselves to be able to contribute to this world in a way that will make Hashem proud. This way, we can still be delighted with achievements, but make sure that we attribute them to the true source.

A few years ago, when I was ill, I lost the ability to speak. I suddenly realised that my words are a gift. Even though I had important things that I wanted to say (well - I thought

We need to recognise our talents, but realise that they come from Hashem.

they were important anyway), Hashem decided that it was not the right time for those words to be released from my mouth.

There is a prayer that we say before the Amidah: "Hashem Sefasai Tiftach, Ufi Yagid Tehilatecha - Hashem, open up my lips, and my mouth will speak your praise." Only when You open my mouth, will the words appear. Now, a few years later, I humbly thank Hashem for that gift and hope and pray that I use those words wisely.

As we celebrate Shavuot together, let us remember our talents, thank Hashem for them, and think about how we can use them to help others and bring joy to the world.

Why Do We Worry?

JUNE 2021

I have been surrounded by problems all my life, but the curious thing about them is that nine-tenths of them never happened."

Andrew Carnegie.

I love this quote. It makes me smile and when I am in a place of worry or fear it brings me back to the real world.

No-one chooses to worry. The worrying thought pops up in the brain and it's very hard to uproot it. Other people telling you not to worry doesn't help either. Worrying is often not logical, but emotional.

So how can we help ourselves, when worrying thoughts enter our minds?

Most worries are about possible future events. Dr Robert L Leahy[*] described a study in which subjects were asked to write down their worries over an extended period of time and then identify which of their imagined misfortunes did not actually happen. It transpired that 85% of what the subjects worried about never happened. And with the 15% of events that did happen, 79% of subjects discovered either that they could handle the difficulty better than expected, or that the difficulty taught them a lesson worth learning. This means that 97% of what one worries about is not much more than a fearful mind filled with exaggerations and misperceptions.

When anticipating new experiences, it is natural to worry about how we will acclimatise to the new situation. Fear of the unknown can be crippling, and the truth is that we do not know how well we will cope until we are actually in that situation.

Rabbi Ashear, a young rabbi from America, taught that Hashem only gives us the tools to deal with a situation once we are in it. So when we are thinking about it in advance, we don't have those tools in place. Thus it seems to us that we may not be able to deal with the challenge.

In Parshat Shelach Lecha, the Jews fear leaving the desert (with Hashem's loving protection) and entering the land of Israel. They were worried about whether or not they would survive the transition and whether Hashem would still help them once they were settled in their own country. This fear was unfounded, as Hashem had promised to remain with them and grant them success.

The Jews sent spies to check out the land, and they returned with upsetting news. "The people were giants," they cried, and "the earth consumes its inhabitants" (Numbers 13:32–33). What made them think

---

[*] *Dr Robert L Leahy is a psychologist and the author and editor of 28 books dedicated to cognitive behaviour therapy. He is Director of the American Institute for Cognitive Therapy in New York and Clinical Professor of Psychology in the Department of Psychiatry at Weill Cornell Medical College.*

that the earth was uninhabitable?

The great medieval commentator, Rashi, explains that whilst they were spying the land, there were a large number of funerals. Hashem had orchestrated these events so that the natives would be occupied and not notice the incoming spies. However, the spies only saw the funerals, and mistook the situation to mean that the land was unfit for humans. Their fears skewed their vision and left them full of unwarranted concerns, which led to their own downfall. Unfortunately, those who believed the spies did not merit to enter the land, for they lacked the requisite faith to endure the transition. On the other hand, those who worked on their faith in Hashem, and trusted that Hashem would keep them safe as promised, found that those potential problems never actually happened.

> *97% of what one worries about is not much more than a fearful mind filled with exaggerations and misperceptions.*

The news and media are full of possible problems that we may encounter. Whilst it is true that any of those problems could occur, it is also highly likely that they will not. It is not easy to switch off the mind from worrying thoughts, but enhancing one's faith in Hashem can help to give us peace of mind, which will enable us to live with hope rather than fear.

Oops! I Forgot to Read the Small Print

PARSHAT CHUKAT, JUNE 2021

When buying online, we are inundated with amazing deals, fantastic products and air-brushed results. We want what these people have and press the 'Buy' button in the hope that we will experience the same results as those we see in the advert. The small print, though, is often ignored or overlooked.

The small print reflects the details – the limitations, the instructions and the possible consequences of misuse. But who has the time to read through all the boring minutiae? Does it really matter anyway?

Anyone who has made purchases over the internet will agree that ignoring the small print can cause a frustrating loss of money and time. I know this because I recently signed up to a free trial and forgot to cancel the subscription after the trial period ended.

In Parshat Chukat, the Torah teaches us about spiritual impurity and the laws of the red heifer. It all seems so archaic and irrelevant to our lives nowadays. Do we really need to follow the exact protocol in order to remove spiritual impurity? Why can't we just say a few words and become pure again?

Spirituality is not just airy-fairy ideas. Hashem's guidelines are clear and precise, for our actions have consequences far beyond what we see at the time.

This law is called a 'chok' in Hebrew – a law for which no reason is given and that we cannot understand. As mere mortal human beings, we cannot fully comprehend the inner workings of this world, and we often make our decisions based on our limited knowledge. Hashem, who created the world, wrote all these details in the Torah – in the small print. It is there for us to read and it is worthwhile for us to follow.

Spirituality is not just airy-fairy ideas. Hashem's guidelines are clear and precise, for our actions have consequences far beyond what we see at the time.

Imagine a friend asks you to send her an email and gives you her email address. You write the email but mistakenly leave out one letter of the address. The email will bounce back. However beautiful your words are in the email, it will not help, for the email address must be 100% correct in order for it to reach its destination. Even if we don't understand the inner workings of a computer, we need to pay attention to details if we want the email to reach its destination.

Those seemingly minor details are more important than we realise and we would benefit from reading them as best we can. Whilst every detail matters, we are lucky that Hashem is our loving Parent, who values every attempt of ours to follow Hashem's laws. Unlike an email, we are actually rewarded for just reading through the instructions and trying our best to do the mitzvot.

If you can, this Shabbat, why not take a few minutes to read some Torah thoughts and perhaps you will find yourself enlightened by the 'small print'.

It's a Secret

PARSHAT BALAK, JUNE 2021

One rabbi was so addicted to golf that he snuck out to play between the morning and afternoon services of Yom Kippur. Up in Heaven, Moses said, "What a disgrace! A Jew playing golf on Yom Kippur? And a rabbi to boot!" The Almighty responded, "I'm going to teach him a lesson."

Out on the course, the rabbi stepped up to the first tee and bombed his drive down the fairway. His ball bounced off a sprinkler head, cart path and bunker rake, hit the green and rolled into the cup.

"This is how You teach him a lesson, L-rd?" asked Moses. "He got a hole in one!"

"Sure," replied G-d. "But who's he going to tell?!"

We all like to be 'in the know'. We like to hear news about other people's lives, and we are subtly (or not so subtly) encouraged to share our news too. When something positive happens in our life, it feels good to share it with others. Nowadays, the dopamine effect of another's smile or enthusiasm is replaced by the number of 'Likes' that steadily increase on the social media platform where the news was shared.

Either way, we seem to be super-interested in each other's lives and, in this generation, we share far more than our parents and grandparents did. The act of perfecting our public persona (or internet presence) can erode our innate sense of privacy. Not everyone needs to know what I ate for breakfast, and do I really need to know the intricate details of a celebrity's family squabbles?

When the Danish international footballer, Christian Eriksen, collapsed during a football match this week, his fellow Danish players stepped back to allow the medics access and formed a shield around Eriksen to allow him and the tending medics privacy. At this incredibly difficult moment for the footballers, their instinctive reaction was to protect the privacy of their teammate. Thank G-d, he is recovering now and I'm sure he is grateful for their efforts on his behalf.

The act of perfecting our public persona (or internet presence) can erode our innate sense of privacy.

In Parshat Balak, Billam (a non-Jewish prophet) sets out to curse the Jewish people but is surprised when his mouth delivers words of praise instead. "How wonderful are your tents, Jacob, your dwelling places of Israel!" (Numbers 24:5). Rashi explains that the beauty of their dwelling places was the fact that their doorways did not face each other. This enabled families to maintain their own privacy and avoid looking into another's home inadvertently.

Privacy is an important Torah value, both in terms of what we ourselves share and also in terms of what we search for and read about others. Holding back from both may well feel uncomfortable, yet it will help build and strengthen one's inner world, which is ultimately much more important than the latest piece of 'gossip'.

Someone is Watching You!

JUNE 2021

This morning, I woke up and checked my inbox. (I know I shouldn't have my phone next to my bed, but that's an article for another time.)

There was a message there from Google, detailing where I had been over the past month. Fascinating. Did you know that I travelled over 450 miles in just one month? I was quite shocked (and also grateful to Hashem for our car!).

The truth is. though, that I found the email rather creepy. I don't remember all the journeys I took this month, but Google does. It's all recorded and stored somewhere on the internet.

Hashem notices every step we take, every decision we make and every fleeting thought. It is all recorded in a book and, one day, we will read that book.

Google just sent me a reminder of that reality. What will my book look like? What pages will I skip over due to severe embarrassment, and what pages will I linger over with pride?

The good news is that whilst we are here in this world, we can edit the book. Not only today's page, but last week's too. Teshuva, sincere regret and an honest attempt to correct our mistakes, can rewrite the pages of our book. What a huge gift Hashem gave us. And it doesn't only work on Yom Kippur; it can be done any day. We can make amends, we can try again, and we can work on ourselves to fill our book with mitzvot.

Every day, we are writing and rewriting our book. Let us make use of this precious opportunity, and write a book full of thoughts, words and actions that we are sure we will be proud of.

A Friendship Bench

JULY 2021

Shani Avigal is the mother of six-year-old Ido Avigal from Sderot, Israel, who was killed in the recent 'Guardian of the Walls' conflict. She is still healing from her painful loss. Yesterday, she wrote the following to Sivan Rachav Meir, an influential Israeli media personality and lecturer.

"I thought a lot about how to memorialize Ido, how he would want me to memorialize him.

"I thought about the value of friendship and that it was sometimes difficult for him to connect with others. Whether in kindergarten or on a playground, he would play alone and find it difficult to participate in group activities. I thought that if there had been a 'friendship bench' at his kindergarten, that could have been most helpful to him.

"The idea is this: If it is difficult for a child to connect, he can simply sit on the bench and others can approach him and ask him to join their game. If children argue amongst themselves, they can also resolve their arguments on the bench.

"The idea began with one bench at his kindergarten and has now spread to schools and even public parks. A number of cities have already ordered these benches in preparation for the coming school year. The feedback I have been receiving is tremendous. The benches simply help children who are socially isolated or otherwise in distress.

"Every night before bed, Ido would share with us what happened to him that day and said that he always made sure to "love his neighbour as himself". Therefore, this is what is written on the bench."

This Sunday is Tisha B'av, the ninth day of the Jewish month of Av. It is the saddest day of the Jewish calendar. We mourn the destruction of the two Temples in Jerusalem (in the years 586 BCE and 70 CE), and the many other tragedies that took place on that day throughout our history. But if it all happened so long ago, why do we keep on crying and mourning?

If it is difficult for a child to connect, he can simply sit on the bench and others can approach him and ask him to join their game.

Our rabbis say that "Any generation in which the Temple is not built, it is as if it had been destroyed in their times" (Yerushalmi, Yoma Ia). It is not only due to the faults of previous generations. We still have not corrected the errors of our ancestors and that is why we find ourselves in exile today – with an imperfect world and much suffering.

The Bet Hamikdash (Temple) was destroyed because of 'Sinat Chinam', baseless hatred. It will be rebuilt when we practice 'Ahavat Chinam', baseless love. Extending friendship to others brings people together.

One woman, who suffered a terrible loss, decided to do something that would bring more friendship into the world. It was a small gesture, yet it has already touched so many children. We too can try to think of something small that we could do to build bridges and unite people.

Together let us build more friendship and, please G-d, may we merit that this year, rather than mourning the loss, we will be celebrating the rebuilding of the Temple. May it be speedily and in our days.

Changing the Narrative

JULY 2021

I recently read a story by Rabbi Benzion Klasko, a young rabbi from America, and it touched me so much. I hope it will touch you too.

The world often looks at us in certain ways and is quick to apply condescending labels – money-hungry, separatists – but we should be just as quick to show them how their narrative of us Jews is wrong.

I was at a house sale some time ago, where I spotted a beautiful piano. Both my wife and I had grown up with pianos, and I figured that it would be a nice piece of furniture to add to our home and be used to play. Turning to the man running the sale, I asked for the price. "$250 in cash," he said. I knew immediately that $250 was a superb price for a good piano and showed interest in buying it. "The only thing is that a lady came here before you and was asking about it. It looks like she is going to buy it." I turned around and soon spotted the woman who had shown such interest. "No problem," I replied to the proprietor, "she came first and has the preferred right to purchase it." "But wait just one minute here," added the owner, "let's just make sure that she has the money."

Checking with the woman that she had the $250 in cash on hand to buy the piano, she said that she would take a look. If she didn't have it, she offered to go home and bring the money right away. Turning to me, he asked if I had the money readily available. "I do have the cash," I said, "but I am not going to jump in front of her." "Why?" the man asked me in curious disbelief. "You have the cash! I'll sell it to you, and it'll be a done deal."

Before he could go any further, I interjected. "I can't do that," I said. "In Judaism, we have a concept which teaches that if a person enters into a transactional agreement with someone and settles on a price, even though no transaction has actually been completed, no one else can interfere and try to purchase the item for themselves (in the language of our rabbis, this is termed, "ani hamehapech b'charara", an impoverished person chasing a crust of bread.) Here this woman has agreed to pay the settled price of $250; I can't jump in and grab the deal."

But the owner didn't understand and couldn't grasp the fact that I was so politely allowing her to buy the piano and stepping aside myself. "Do you have the money or not?" he asked the woman again. She opened up her purse, and including singles, had a total of $70. The man turned back to me. "Look, she doesn't have the money!" "I can go home," she said. "Ma'am," firmly said the owner, "I can't afford to lose a customer if I have to wait for you while you return home."

I then turned to the woman, and said, "How much more do you need? Another $180?" I opened my wallet, counted out $180 and handed it to her. "Take this," I said, "I'll give you my address and you can send me the money when you get back home."

The owner couldn't believe his eyes. What about the Jewish narrative that we are cheap, stingy and selfish? "Do you even know this lady?" he asked. "No, I replied, "but I trust that she will return the money to me as soon as she has the opportunity." And that was it. I then proceeded to walk into one of the adjacent rooms.

Just minutes later, one of the young helpers came running over to me. "Do you know what they're saying about you out there? They're so impressed. They said that they realize now that they've never understood Jews!"

Reflecting on this, I realized that here was an opportunity to not only make a Kiddush Hashem (sanctification Hashem's name), but to also change the narrative that the world has of Jews.

The story has a very interesting ending though.

As I was about to leave, I noticed that there were a few bottles of wine and alcohol for sale. "How much are these?" I asked. The owner looked at me and said, "They're yours." "No, no, I don't want them for free," I made clear. "How much are they?" "They're yours. I want you to have them."

The owner certainly had the right to freely give them to me, and so I graciously complied. After taking them and returning home, I discovered that one was a $300 bottle of Scotch, the other was a bottle of Cherry Heering Liqueur that was about 50 years old, and the third was a bottle of Sabra liqueur from the 1960s. They were all collectors' items and worth more than the piano I had let go.

Even if that was not the ending of the story, the lesson for us is to realise the tremendous opportunity we have to create a lasting impression with our actions. We do not simply inspire others by our caring and thoughtful actions; we change people's narrative of the Jews and offer the world new lenses through which to view us in a much more positive light.

May we merit to be the kind of people who inspire all those we meet.

What Are You Bringing With?

AUGUST 2021

A few weeks ago, there was a terrible fire in the Jerusalem Hills. Many homes were destroyed and factories and warehouses burnt to the ground. Our thoughts and prayers are with those who lost their homes and businesses.

Sivan Rachav Meir shared a thought written by one of the residents of the nearby villages, David Saada.

"My wife and I recently moved into Moshav Beit Meir and today we were forced to leave due to the huge fire in the Jerusalem hills. It is difficult to describe the feeling when you see black smoke clouds outside your home and they are telling you that you must evacuate. And you ask yourself: what is most important to take with you? All your life goes smoothly and suddenly you have just a few moments to ask: what is most valuable to you? It's about survival and it's frightening. I said to myself that I will leave here with just a few items and return to see all the rest of my possessions destroyed.

What would I take with? What item in my home is most precious to me? And why?

"Now, as I relive those last few seconds, I recall taking my tallit, tefillin, a few holy books, some books of Rav Nachman, the guitars and the cats. We left in our car in a panic, after making sure our neighbours were alright. We drove through a cloud of smoke while flames threatened to burn down our house.

"Baruch Hashem, we are okay. We are staying with my mother-in-law, our house is also okay, but it was still an earth-shattering experience. We received a 'jolt' for the month of Elul as we were compelled to ask ourselves: what is most important in life?"

It made me think. What would I take with? What item in my home is most precious to me? And why?

We recently returned from a short holiday in England. Packing for seven people is quite a big job and we needed to bring cooking utensils, pots and pans. Yet even with all those suitcases, we still only took with us a fraction of what we own. When I came home, I looked around and wondered why we have so much 'stuff'. Do we really need all these items?

In Ethics of Our Fathers (2:8), our rabbis wrote "Marbeh nechasim, marbeh da'aga"; the more possessions, the more worry.

Living in the 21st century, we are blessed with more 'things' than our ancestors ever dreamed of. The question is: do all these items enhance our lives or do they remove us from our primary goals?

As we are approaching Rosh Hashana, it is a good time to look around our homes and take stock of our belongings. Do they work for us or do we work for them?

If we look a little deeper, we may be surprised with our answers.

Beware: Mouth Guards

AUGUST 2021

I hope you are having a nice summer.

Thank you to all those who joined us for Devorah and Mischa's wedding, and we missed those who were unable to be there. May we always share simchas together.

It feels like I haven't written for ages, and although we have been quite busy with the wedding and summer plans, I have missed you all!

Could you imagine what life would be like if we had guards on our mouths?

Due to the coronavirus, many of us know the feeling of having a mask over our face, but this is something different.

Imagine how we would feel if we had a sensor placed on our lips that would prevent harmful words from passing through. If such a product was available, would we want to buy it?

So many of our troubles are due to words that we spoke intentionally and unintentionally. Perhaps we were angry and we spoke harsher words than necessary, or maybe we were just chatting innocently but didn't realise that we had shared something that should have been kept private.

It seems like words are just air, but in reality, words have the power to inflict tremendous harm or produce incredibly positive feelings for another person.

On his "Desert Island Discs" interview on Radio 4, the former footballer Ian Wright spoke about a teacher who encouraged him and believed in him when no-one else did. This teacher lifted Ian from the depths of despair and gave him a reason to keep on trying.

In this week's Parsha, our greatest teacher, Moshe, tells us to "Place judges and policemen for your gates" (Deuteronomy 16:18). The literal translation is to set up a fair legal and law enforcement system for the community.

Looking a little deeper, the Shelah (1555–1630, a prominent rabbi and mystic)* translates this homiletically as follows. The gates mentioned in the Torah verse allude to the personal 'gates' of the human body: the seven orifices that are a conduit to four of the five senses, namely our two ears, two eyes, two nostrils and a mouth.

Hashem created the mouth with two 'natural' guards – the teeth and the lips. Before opening our mouths and sharing our thoughts, those two levels of protection need to be unlocked.

In other words, be careful with what you see, with what you hear and with the words that come out of your mouth.

Next week, we will look at what we see and hear, but this week I'd like to focus on our mouths.

Hashem created the mouth with two 'natural' guards – the teeth and the lips. Before opening our mouths and sharing our thoughts, those two levels of protection need to be unlocked.

We may not even realise it, for our words often escape without much thought, and quick wittedness is considered praiseworthy in our current society. You may notice, though, that truly wise people tend to speak more slowly and with more forethought.

I remember learning this sweet poem when I was a child, and it is still as relevant as ever.

"Be careful of the words you say,
Keep them soft and sweet
You never know from day to day
Which ones you'll have to eat".
(Author unknown)

For those of us who are blessed to have the ability to speak, let us remember to guard and protect this gift and ensure that the words we speak are ones we would love to hear spoken to us.

* The Shelah Hakadosh was Isaiah ben Avraham Ha-Levi Horowitz. He was born in Prague, became a rabbi in Austria and then moved to Jerusalem. He was one of the 15 rabbis kidnapped for ransom in 1625 and he moved to Safed, Israel, when he was released. He is buried in Tiberias.

As we enter the month of Ellul (and there are 26 days left until Rosh Hashana), it is customary to think back over the year and try to repair any mistakes before the Day of Judgement. Together, let us work on our words so that we will all merit a year full of blessings and positivity.

"I'm Not Religious"

SEPTEMBER 2021

You may be thinking that this is a slightly odd statement coming from a United Synagogue Reb-betzen.

Please allow me to explain myself.

One of my favourite parts of my job is meeting lots of different people. Each person is like a whole world and I'm always fascinated to learn about other people's lives and experiences.

When discussing shul, people will often say to me "I'm not religious, but ...". I often wonder why they feel the need to share this piece of information with me. Please correct me if I am wrong, but it feels like this statement separates us with a wall: "You are religious and I am not". Yet, I see you as my brother or sister. We are all one family, with a Parent who loves us all.

Was does the world 'religious' actually mean, anyway?

According to Merriam-Webster, it means "relating to or manifesting faithful devotion to an acknowledged ultimate reality or deity."

Everyone has their own private relationship with Hashem, even those who may identify as 'not religious'. Some may be upset with Hashem, or feel that they can't understand Hashem's ways (who can?), but we are all still Hashem's children.

Hashem gave to Torah to all the Jewish people. You and me. Hashem gave it to us with love, and we are rewarded for each and every mitzva we perform. Some mitzvot are easier than others, but many of us do mitzvot every day without realising that they are actually mitzvot.

Are you honest in business? Do you respect your parents? Do you give charity to those who need? All these are mitzvot from the Torah and even someone who does not classify themselves as religious is already performing many mitzvot. Hashem has an open door for anyone who wants to come close, at any time.

A while ago, I gave the parable of a farmer who had a chance to collect precious gold stones from the dungeons of the king's palace (see page 49). The farmer was too busy enjoying the scenery to pick up the precious stones and was so disappointed with himself when his time was up and he realised what an opportunity he had missed.

We need to set ourselves up for success

The mitzvot are like precious gold coins, and we only have limited time here on this earth to collect them. They are lying on the floor, free for all of to pick up, whether we are religious or not. Of course, we all have free choice as to whether we want to recognise the precious stones' beauty, or if we prefer to ignore them.

I just feel that labels are harmful and sometimes prevent us from growing in ways that could benefit us. Judaism is not all or nothing. Making a bracha (blessing) on food before eating does not change one's identity, but it is an easy mitzva that lifts the simple act of eating into a Divine act of appreciation. Similarly, celebrating the gift of Shabbat is open to all of us, no matter where we place ourselves on the religious spectrum. Making Kiddush on a cup of wine, eating a lovely meal and turning off the constant noise for one day a week, rejuvenates us – not only spiritually but also physically.

When we label ourselves ("I'm no good at singing" or "I'm so clumsy - I'll probably break it"), we lock ourselves in. Human beings have the potential to change and to flourish. Perhaps we could remove our self-limiting box and give ourselves that full opportunity to embrace our identity as Jews, and our ability to connect each day with the Divine.

Am I Insane?

SEPTEMBER 2021

Just to clarify, the title was a rhetorical question. I'd rather you don't respond, thanks!

Generally, I think I'm quite normal, but I recently read a definition of insanity that made me question myself.

> ### *"Insanity is doing the same thing over and over and expecting to get different results."*
>
> *Albert Einstein*

Sounds a bit like my yearly Rosh Hashana experience.... Here's the scenario.

Summer holidays are busy, then the new school year begins and suddenly Rosh Hashana arrives. I begin to get a little nervous, thinking about how important this special day is, and start to do a 'cheshbon hanefesh', spiritual accounting of myself.

As I think back over the year, I try to remember my last New Year's resolutions, and fail. I look at my faults to see if they have improved and find that they are still there in full force. It is a bit depressing really.

If I feel the same way every year, something needs to change. Nothing changes if nothing changes. Good intentions coupled with some vague plans are not enough to help a person change.

Marshall Goldsmith writes about this phenomena in his book, "Triggers". Human beings suffer from inertia. We'd much prefer to do nothing rather than work on ourselves, and Rabbi Salanter said that repairing one bad character trait is more difficult than learning the entire Talmud.

So what is the answer? Am I doomed to insanity?

If one was preparing for a business proposal, it would not be enough to arrive at the meeting with a great vision. A good proposal would also contain clear practical steps as to how to achieve that vision.

We need to approach our Rosh Hashana resolutions with the same mindset. Looking at our lives, we need to identify what we want to change, and what steps we can take that will enable us to accomplish those goals.

One idea suggested by Goldsmith is that our environment is much more powerful than we realise, and it often affects us so subtly that we are unaware of its influence. He writes "If we do not create and control our environment, our environment creates and controls us. And the result turns us into someone we do not recognise". If we analyse our behaviour, we will see that we behave differently depending on the environment. Some people bring out the best in us, and others do not.

> *"Insanity is doing the same thing over and over and expecting to get different results."*

When making a plan to improve, we need to set ourselves up for success by working on placing ourselves in an environment that is conducive to growth. Choose your friends carefully, avoid those supermarket aisles containing items you'd rather not consume, and fill your home with inspiring reading and viewing material.

Just as our rabbis taught us many years ago, Goldsmith also advises us to create a daily accounting system, together with a friend. With small manageable, quantifiable goals and a system that holds a person accountable, these grand New Year's resolutions have a greater chance of being achieved.

May we all succeed in our meaningful goals, and may Hashem bless us with a year full of good health, success and happiness.

I Can See a Rainbow

PARSHAT NOACH, OCTOBER 2021

Do you have someone in your life that annoys you? You just don't get along so well, or their general outlook or attitude frustrates you?

We are surrounded by many different people and it is normal for us to occasionally be aggravated by friends or family or work colleagues. The question is, how do we view these people?

"She is just so difficult. There is always something for her to complain about."

"Every time he enters the room, my blood pressure rises. His negativity drives me mad!"

It is hard to find good in people who just seem to carry a black cloud with them wherever they go.

In this week's parsha, we learn about how Hashem brought a flood upon the world and saved only Noah, his family and the animals. When Noah left the Ark after all the destruction, Hashem showed him a rainbow and promised that there would never be a flood again upon the whole world.

What actually is a rainbow?

According to Wikipedia, a rainbow is "a meteorological phenomenon that is caused by reflection, refraction and dispersion of light in water droplets resulting in a spectrum of light appearing in the sky. It takes the form of a multicoloured circular arc".

In other words, when the sun hits a dark black cloud in a storm, the light is refracted through the cloud and a beautiful spectrum of colours shines through into the sky.

120 years before the flood, Noah was told to start building the Ark. He was also told to warn the people about the flood and encourage them to repair their evil ways. As Rabbi Bernstein zt"l so beautifully quipped, "120 years of the same sermon and not one convert. That must be grounds for dismissal!". Every day, Noah told the people the same message, but no one listened and no one changed.

When Hashem showed Noah the rainbow, Hashem was teaching him an important lesson. Even though Noah relayed the message, he did not see the good in the people of that generation. He saw them as hopeless sinners and therefore his words had no effect on them. Hashem was showing Noah that if you shine a light on the dark cloud, if you believe in someone's innate goodness, then beautiful colours can emerge from within that cloud.

We all like to be around people who emit brightness and joy like the sun. The harder task is to look for those colours within the 'dark clouds' and help bring out the beauty from within those drops of water. All it takes is to shine some of our own light onto them and give them hope in themselves. Had Noah believed in the potential of those in that generation, perhaps more people would have been saved in the Ark.

When Noah left the Ark after all the destruction, Hashem showed him a rainbow and promised that there would never be a flood again upon the whole world.

As we sit in our homes this Shabbat, let us try to think about those people who frustrate us and see if we can find some goodness in them and give them some light, so that they too will radiate beautiful colours upon the world.

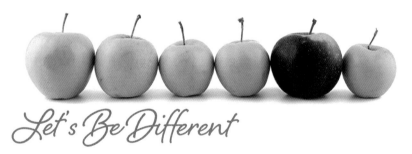

Let's Be Different

OCTOBER 2021

Imagine walking into a room full of people. Most likely, you will look around for someone you know or a friend with whom you can chat.

We are social beings and we long to be accepted and respected by those around us.

Abraham lived during an era where polytheism was the prevailing worldview. People worshipped idols, and prayed to different stone creations in order to placate the various gods.

Abraham's father was actually a stone mason who owned a shop full of idols, which he created himself and sold to customers in order to make a living.

Abraham, though, was an inquisitive child. He looked around at the world and could not understand how this incredible, beautiful, complex world could be created by stones that humans produced themselves!

He searched and searched for the answer to this question and looked for the creator. When Hashem saw Abraham's sincerity, Hashem spoke to him and told him to leave his birthplace.

At this point, Abraham became "Ha'ivri", the first "Hebrew". The world 'ivri' means '(from) the other side'. The whole world believed in one idea and he believed something else. It must have been quite a lonely place for Abraham. Yet he maintained his belief and followed Hashem into a world that was totally unfamiliar.

> *No one likes to be too different, and Abraham was challenged by many critics, but due to his tenacity his legacy continues in us.*

Abraham was thrown into a fire, sent to a land where there was a famine and had his wife kidnapped by a king. Not exactly an easy life! Hashem promised that he would become a great nation, but all Abraham saw were life's tests. Despite all of this, he still remained 'on the other side'. Many years later, we are still reaping the benefits of his individual choice. Through Isaac, his son, he did eventually grow into a great nation. Not great in size, but great in its ambitions.

No one likes to be too different, and Abraham was challenged by many critics, but due to his tenacity his legacy continues in us.

Living in the 21st century brings us different challenges to those faced by Abraham. We are lucky enough to live in a society that accepts diverse belief systems, rather than forbidding them. Our challenge is to embrace our Judaism, even though we do not need to fight for it. The social pressures still exist – albeit in a varied format. We want acceptance from our friends, colleagues and neighbours. Living differently takes courage and strength, even in our day and age.

Whilst travelling along our life's journey, let us remember Abraham's choices and use that inspiration to guide the decisions we make ourselves.

Please Don't Tell Me What To Do

OCTOBER 2021

No one likes being told what to do.

I've noticed this over the years, when I have nagged the children to clean up their room and find myself frustrated with their lack of enthusiasm for the task.

We all have great ideas. Sometimes, those ideas hit us with a powerful force of excitement. We just want everyone else to know about it and follow our amazing plans!

More often than not, though, these ideas are met with scepticism by those who don't share our vision. This can be disheartening, as our bubble of brilliance is popped.

So, what is the best way to influence others?

Our job in this world, as the Jewish nation, is to be "a light for the nations" and inspire others to recognise Hashem and create a moral, helpful, giving and peaceful society.

When we welcome guests into our home, offering them hospitality and love, we follow in Abraham's footsteps.

How can we do this?

Last week, we spoke about Abraham's epiphany. He discovered Hashem, and wanted desperately to share that new knowledge with the world. As Rabbi Sacks wrote in 2013, "Abraham is without doubt the most influential person who ever lived. Today he is claimed as the spiritual ancestor of 2.3 billion Christians, 1.8 billion Muslims and 14 million Jews, more than half the people alive today. Yet he ruled no empire, commanded no great army, performed no miracles and proclaimed no prophecy. He is the supreme example in all of history of influence without power."

So, let's find out how he accomplished such a great feat...

The Midrash explains that Abraham opened his home to travellers who needed a place to rest and eat. He served them with joy and gave them the finest foods he could prepare. When the visitors finished their food and had a rest, they asked how much they owed him. Abraham replied, "There is no need to pay me, just thank Hashem, who has blessed me with the ability to give." They asked who Hashem was, and he explained that there was one G-d who created the world.

Through giving to others freely, he personally embodied the attributes of Hashem. He didn't tell them to be givers, he didn't scream his ideas from the rooftops, he merely led by personal example and, when asked about his kindness, he shared his worldview.

Abraham passed all ten of his own tests, with flying colours. He followed Hashem's orders even when he didn't understand them or see positive results. He worked on himself every day to fulfil the will of his Creator, and yet he was full of love and patience for others who were not doing so themselves.

That is how to lead. Through personal example and an open and (for) giving attitude.

When we welcome guests into our home, offering them hospitality and love, we follow in Abraham's footsteps.

Due to the coronavirus, we have all been more cautious about inviting guests, but there are other ways to 'welcome' others into our lives. Sending a warm, encouraging text message; smiling to our service providers; allowing someone else to go in front of you in the supermarket and any other random acts of kindness, all influence the world in a positive way.

When I write these messages, I am also talking to myself... So next time I feel the urge to share some good advice for living (or tell someone else what to do!), I will try to focus instead on leading by example.

Save Me From The Selfie

DECEMBER 2021

Are you a fan of taking pictures? Personally, I'd rather leave my camera (and phone too) at home and enjoy the experience. However, I understand how looking at photos enhances the positive memories and therefore I often nag everyone to stop and smile, so that we can relive this moment another time.

Cameras have evolved though, and we now have more exciting options – like selfies. In the olden days (I'm sounding old...), we took pictures of others. Nowadays, we take pictures of ourselves. Although I like the memories, I really do not enjoy taking pictures of myself. That's why I stand behind the camera.

By 2013, the word 'selfie' had become commonplace enough to be monitored for inclusion in the online version of the Oxford English Dictionary, which announced it as the 'word of the year' in November, with an Australian origin. In August 2014, 'selfie' was officially accepted for use in the word game Scrabble.

What worries me about this word is that it signifies a shift in focus for humankind. The focus has become 'me', rather than 'us'. (I wonder if the names iPhone, iPod and iPad are just coincidences?)

As Rabbi Sacks, of blessed memory, wrote "The contemporary west is the most individualistic era of all time. Its central values are in ethics, autonomy; in politics, individual rights; in culture, post-modernism...Its idol is the self and its icon the selfie" ("Not in God's Name", page 41).

When discussing with teenagers their hopes and dreams, I often hear how they want to climb a mountain, become a famous actress or some similar great achievement. They are encouraged to follow their dreams and find what gives them a sense of self-fulfilment.

In Judaism, our goal is not self-fulfilment; it is our contribution of self.

Our aspirations are less about what is best for me, and more about what will be best for society as a whole. Although, Hillel famously asked, "If I am not for me, who am I?", he made sure to follow it with "and if I am only for myself, then what am I?" (Ethics of Our Fathers 1:14)

In this week's parsha, Moshe is born, adopted by Pharaoh's daughter and living the life of luxury in Pharaoh's palace. If he was thinking about his own personal potential for success, he could have risen to high places within the palace. Yet his focus was on his people, and their suffering. Parenthetically, it was this caring that was the catalyst for him becoming the leader of his people.

> *... the more we concentrate on our own fulfilment and happiness, the more miserable we are...*

But this was not his goal. He walked around the Jewish slave labour building sites, and tried his best to alleviate some of his brothers' and sisters' pain.

Paradoxically, the more we concentrate on our own fulfilment and happiness, the more miserable we are, whereas the more we think about how we can help others, the happier we feel.

If each one of us try to shift our focus from I to we, then together we will all find true fulfilment.

GLOSSARY

Bashert . . . . A Jewish expression meaning 'it was meant to happen'.

Chag . . . . The Hebrew word for 'festival'.

Chanuka . . . . The festival of lights, celebrated for eight days in the Jewish month of Kisleiv (in the winter), commemorating the miracle of the small jug of oil that stayed alight for eight nights, after the Jews tried to restore their Temple in Jerusalem that the Syrian Greeks had defiled (138 BCE).

Chassidut . . . . . . A movement within Judaism founded by the 'Baal Shem Tov' in 1736. It emphasized prayer, joy and kabbalah (Jewish mysticism).

Hashem . . . . Literally 'The Name'. The Hebrew word used for G-d in non-sacred language.

Mitzva . . . . Often translated as 'good deed', the word actually means 'instruction'.

Mitzvot . . . . There are 613 mitzvot (instructions) in the Torah.

Nachas . . . . Pride or gratification, especially at the achievements of one's children or students.

Pesach . . . . The Passover festival that commemorates the miraculous escape of the Jews from Egypt, after 210 years of slavery (1313 BCE).

Purim . . . . The festival that commemorates the evil plans of Haman in Persia, and how Hashem saved us from destruction through Queen Esther, and her uncle Mordechai. (355 BCE)

Rosh Hashana . . The Jewish New Year, celebrated in the Jewish month of Tishrei (in the autumn).

Seder . . . . A special evening on the first and second night of Passover, where we retell the story of what happened to our people in Egypt, using matza (unleavened bread), four cups of wine and maror (bitter herbs).

Shabbat .... The Jewish weekly festival that commemorates how Hashem created the world in six days and rested on the seventh. It begins on Friday before sunset and ends on Saturday after nightfall. Shabbat is celebrated with wine, challa (bread), festive meals, prayer and family time.

Succah......... A temporary hut, open to the sky, with leaves for the roof. We dwell in it for seven (or eight in the Diaspora) days to commemorate how Hashem looked after us for 40 years in the desert before entering the Land of Israel.

Succot .... The festival in which we dwell in the Succah, refrain from work, shake the Arba Minim (four species) and have festive meals with family and friends.

Tefilla.......... Prayer

Teshuva .... Literally 'coming back'. It is a process which Hashem gave us to enable us to return when we err. The process entails stopping the wrong behaviour, admitting the mistake, making amends and planning to improve in the future.

Torah.......... The Five Books of Moshe (Genesis, Exodus, Leviticus, Numbers and Deuteronomy), given to the Jewish people at Mount Sinai, which contains our instructions for life.

Tzedaka .... Charity

Yom Kippur .... The Day of Atonement. A day spent fasting, praying and asking Hashem to forgive us.